Competitive Karate

Adam Gibson

Bill "Superfoot" Wallace

Human Kinetics

Library of Congress Cataloging-in-Publication Data

Gibson, Adam.
  Competitive karate / Adam Gibson, Bill "Superfoot" Wallace.
    p. cm.
Includes index.
  ISBN 0-7360-4492-2 (Soft cover)
  1. Karate. I. Wallace, Bill, 1945-   II. Title.
  GV1114.3.G53   2004
  796.815'3--dc22
ISBN: 0-7360-4492-2   2003021445

The Web addresses cited in this text were current as of December 1, 2003, unless otherwise noted.

Acquisitions Editor: Ed McNeely; **Developmental Editor:** Julie Rhoda; **Assistant Editors:** Alisha Jeddeloh, Kim Thoren, and Carla Zych; **Copyeditors:** Jan Feeney and Carla Zych; **Proofreader:** Joanna Hatzopoulos Portman; **Indexer:** Nan N. Badgett; **Graphic Designer:** Nancy Rasmus; **Graphic Artist:** Sandra Meier; **Photo Manager:** Dan Wendt; **Cover Designer:** Jack W. Davis; **Photographer (cover):** © Bongarts/SportsChrome; **Photographer (interior):** André Ringuette/Freestyle Photography; **Printer:** United Graphics

We thank Adam Gibson's Martial Gym in Bowmanville, Ontario, Canada, for providing the location for the photo shoot for this book.

Human Kinetics books are available at special discounts for bulk purchase. Special editions or book excerpts can also be created to specification. For details, contact the Special Sales Manager at Human Kinetics.

Printed in the United States of America

10 9 8 7 6 5 4 3 2 1

Human Kinetics
Web site: www.HumanKinetics.com

United States: Human Kinetics
P.O. Box 5076
Champaign, IL 61825-5076
800-747-4457
e-mail: humank@hkusa.com

Canada: Human Kinetics
475 Devonshire Road Unit 100
Windsor, ON N8Y 2L5
800-465-7301 (in Canada only)
e-mail: orders@hkcanada.com

Europe: Human Kinetics
107 Bradford Road
Stanningley
Leeds LS28 6AT, United Kingdom
+44 (0) 113 255 5665
e-mail: hk@hkeurope.com

Australia: Human Kinetics
57A Price Avenue
Lower Mitcham, South Australia 5062
08 8277 1555
e-mail: liaw@hkaustralia.com

New Zealand: Human Kinetics
Division of Sports Distributors NZ Ltd.
P.O. Box 300 226 Albany
North Shore City
Auckland
0064 9 448 1207
e-mail: blairc@hknewz.com

This book is dedicated to anyone who has had a dream of becoming a champion, becoming famous, or even becoming a legend in the world of the martial arts.

Without such dreams, the greatest martial artists in the world would not exist. Dreams inspire us to excel far beyond what is normally possible. Dreams are your power, your will, and your desire. Without dreams there would be no champions, no legends, and no future for martial arts.

Believe in your dreams, and they will become your reality.

Adam Gibson

Contents

Introduction   vi
Acknowledgments   viii

Part I   Essence of a Karate Competitor

1 Committing to Competition
   Excellence   1

2 Defining and Refining a Style   9

Part II   Mastery of Technical
and Tactical Maneuvers

3 Applying the Seven Essential
   Techniques   15

4 Manipulating the Opponent
   by Drawing and Luring   65

5 Defending and Countering
Kick Combinations   93

6 Beating the Opponent's
Best Punch   119

7 Jamming Opponents in Close   141

Part III   Preparation for Combat

8 Honing the Body for Competition   153

9 Stifling Opponents' Attacks and
Creating Scoring Opportunities   173

Index   179
About the Authors   183

Introduction

Sport karate has become one the most popular forms of martial arts competition. It allows the practitioner a safe, controlled atmosphere in which to test skills against various opponents by using light contact and a point system. In the point system, as soon as the center judge has decided that a point is scored, the bout is stopped to allow the four corner judges to decide whether the point is valid. There is no single, definitive rulebook or governing body of sport karate, so specific rules may vary from competition to competition. A few sport karate tournaments allow kicking to the groin and legs and leg-sweep takedowns, but the majority of tournament officials today do not allow any target areas below the belt. This makes the sport a little less intimidating for new competitors.

Bill Wallace, coauthor of this book, has revolutionized sport karate through his unparalleled accomplishments and innovative fighting style. Not only did he dominate point tournament karate and kickboxing arenas in the 1960s, 1970s, and early 1980s, but he also created a devastating fighting system that evolved out of a knee injury he incurred while training in judo. He tore all the ligaments in his right knee and was only able to kick with his left leg, which he developed sufficiently to earn his ring name of "Superfoot." At seminars Bill jokes about his injury with audiences, explaining, "That's why they call me 'Superfoot' and not 'Superfeet.'"

Over the past 20 years Bill Wallace's fighting system has become the dominant system in sport karate. The rigid techniques of traditional karate have evolved into Bill's seamless approach to offensive and defensive fighting tactics, which use the lead leg and lead arm. The days of the throw-and-hope tactics have come to an end, thanks to the teachings in this book. There is no reason you should have to make up everything yourself. The drills and concepts in this book, which emphasize placing your hand or foot in the right place at the right time, will train your mind and body to force your opponent to make mistakes.

When Bill first started tearing up the point karate tournament circuit in the 1960s and 1970s, the other fighters and so-called experts (masters) said that his style and techniques were incorrect even though he kept beating his competitors. They said it was suicide to fight the way he did. Bill had more than 250 wins in the black belt division, many at national-level events. He beat all the top fighters—those with traditional martial arts backgrounds, those who favored modern techniques, and everyone else in between. How could he beat everyone if his techniques were incorrect? The answer is very simple: His sparring strategies were very advanced, and no one knew how to deal with his unique approach to a match. That's what the art of war is all about. Confuse the enemy, disrupt his timing, and take control. When martial arts were created thousands of years ago, they were not designed for the sake of style and tradition. They were designed to conquer the enemy, end of story. Bill did just that—he designed his own system that people still marvel over.

When full-contact karate was first introduced in 1974, after Bill had already dominated the world of point tournament karate for many years, his competitors said the same thing all over again: "He can't fight like that; he'll get killed. Maybe that worked in point karate, but this is full-contact karate. This is completely different."

Well, Bill did it again. He walked into the full-contact ring with all the same tricks and kicks and a couple of new hand techniques (a hook punch and an uppercut) and shocked the martial arts world again by retiring in 1980 as undefeated world middleweight kickboxing champion. Bill's fighting style in full-contact competitions was almost identical to what he used in point tournaments, and it worked well in both environments. Nobody knew what it was like to get hit by Bill for real . . . until they set foot in the full-contact ring. He was now allowed to show the true command and full potential of his system: *control* and *power*. He showed *control* in the point karate arena and *power* in the full-contact arena. And most important, he showed *strategic prowess* in both.

This book shows martial artists how to approach opponents to create openings quickly and safely with little fear of being countered. It is our goal to show competitors how to defend against the most common kicks and hand techniques used in tournament karate. We will answer the eternal question: "How do I stop my opponent from doing this to me?"

The first two chapters start with what you need to know to commit to excellence in the sport and how to pick the best fighting style for your body type. We teach you how to use an opponent's style against him. Chapters 3 through 7 help you master and apply seven essential techniques. You'll learn how to control a fight, defend against your opponent's best kick and punch combinations, and jam her moves with photographed drills that take you through every scenario imaginable. The strategic preparation that you receive from following the drills, exercises, and concepts in this book will allow you to gain the edge on the competition before you even set foot in the ring. The last three chapters then help you use the skills you've practiced to prepare for combat. We set up a comprehensive training program to prepare you mentally and physically for the ring; we also give you strategies to help you create openings during the fight and score points against any competitor.

The only techniques that are in this book are those that we both have scored with many times in competition and sparring. Bill's thoughts on fight psychology give you insight into the mind of the world's most legendary sport karate champion and undefeated world full-contact karate champion.

When reading this book, focus on the details. We will show you simple moves and ideas that, when combined, make a great fighter. The biggest mistake that a lot of fighters make is memorizing moves for individual situations instead of memorizing concepts that can be used in all situations. Try to get away from robotic thinking: *I'll throw this kick because he threw that punch.* In the chapters that follow, we'll show you a variety of techniques and how they are linked together by correct footwork and body positioning. Remember, 90 percent of karate is mind and 10 percent of it is muscle.

We hope you find this book to be the most educational book on sport karate and sparring. Enjoy your reading, and good luck in your training!

Acknowledgments

With all my heart I thank my friends, family, and students for all their support during the long process of creating this amazing book. I am grateful to the following students for their appearance in the pages to come: Jean-Guy LaFrance, Paul Edwards, Tyler Bowler, Lara Couch, David McFaul, Kevin Cook, Darla Vallieres, and Trudy Bennett.

I would also like to give special thanks to my friend, my teacher, my mentor, and my coauthor, Bill "Superfoot" Wallace—my life and universe would not be the same without him.

Adam Gibson

1

Committing to Competition Excellence

One of the toughest lessons in life for most people to learn is that the key to true success usually is not based on inborn skills. We have met countless truly gifted people who are their own biggest enemies. These same people are sometimes the most negative and unaware of all of us when it comes to doing the work needed to succeed. They seem to give up the quickest. Because things come so easy to them, they are often not willing to work as hard as someone with less natural skill.

Contrary to popular belief, the people who are most successful are those with average minds and bodies. The one thing that separates them from the crowd is their relentless commitment to their crystal-clear vision, no matter what the consequences. By crystal-clear vision, we mean that they can see themselves reaching their goals, whether it's crossing the finish line before everyone else or standing on the podium in the first-place position.

Committed people always set a goal well in advance and continue to strive for their objectives even if they fall flat on their face attempting to do so. Each time they fall, they get back up and go after their goal until they succeed. Have you ever heard of someone becoming an astronaut or a brain surgeon without being truly committed to the idea of being in such a profession? Did that person get the job by accident or through luck? No. That person got there through sheer will and desire, through sacrifices and hard work. You can have two people of equal intelligence and equal physical abilities, and the one with the most positive attitude and commitment to a goal will be the most successful in life. This is the kind of commitment that is necessary for excelling in sport karate.

This chapter discusses the fundamental characteristics—the sacrifices and drives—that make a great sport karate competitor. It will help you determine how to assess your readiness to start competing in sport karate tournaments. Then you will set goals to help you turn your weaknesses into strengths.

Guided action and positive thinking are the most powerful tools to success in and out of the ring.

WHAT MAKES A GREAT COMPETITOR?

Accomplishing anything really big in life requires a lot of time (usually measured in years), a lot of patience, extreme effort, faithful dedication, a positive attitude, lots of thinking and rethinking the plans of action, and true love of and desire for what you are trying to accomplish.

Commitment to Time and Training

When it comes to martial arts training, levels of commitment can vary greatly. Some people get into it to exercise or to learn some self-defense training, and some get into it to become champion fighters. The commitment required for the average person participating in a martial arts course usually is very minimal to acquire some fitness and basic self-defense training benefits—60 to 90 minutes, two to three times per week. But when it comes to training to become a champion, we are talking about an entirely different commitment—90 minutes per session at least five times a week.

As a champion in training, you're likely to spend most of your training sessions alone because not many other people want to train that many hours. (For more detailed information on suggested amount of training and programs for competitive sparring, see chapter 8.)

Ironically, many tournament participants who talk most about becoming a champion fighter train less than those who have no wish to set foot in a competition. These big talkers show up to a competition completely unprepared but expect to win; therefore, they fail. I have witnessed a lot of these types of people who win first-place trophies in the color belt divisions and, amazingly, do not work out for months before the tournament. But it all finally catches up with them when they hit black belt level at the state or provincial level, the national level, or higher. At these levels the competitors are doing their homework and are trained fighters, not naturals. They have

© Raw Talent Photo

Advanced level black-belt sparring.

3

more advanced strategies and experience. And they have conditioned their minds and bodies for a variety of situations and environments. To survive at this level your commitment must be 100 percent or you will have very little chance of winning.

Training to become a champion will definitely take much of your free time, depending on your school or work schedule. Friends and family may become upset with you and think you are avoiding or ignoring them. Or they might actually believe you're obsessed with your training. This may be an unavoidable situation, and the best thing you can do is to reassure those around you that you still care about them. Let them know that this is something you have decided to commit to and therefore need to spend time training for and that you hope they will understand. Don't let other people's complaints stand in the way of your dreams, unless there is some extreme situation that requires your attention.

Time and Money

When Bill Wallace was competing he claimed more than 250 first-place wins in tournaments all the way to national level. By today's standards, 250 tournaments is a lot, but back then it was a lot less expensive to compete. Some tournaments in the 1960s only cost $5 to enter. Times have changed drastically. It is quite easy now to spend $300 to $500 in a weekend competing, after you add up travel expenses, food, accommodations, and competitor fees. Some tournaments also expect that you pay an association fee or they will not allow you to compete. Tuition fees for classes at modern martial arts schools are ranging from $80 to $140 per month. Unless you're wealthy, or Mom and Dad pay for everything, you may have to budget yourself accordingly by being very selective about the tournaments you attend.

Another issue is time. Most people do not have the time to compete every weekend or every other weekend. Choose tournaments that mean something and will benefit you most in the long run.

Balancing life's daily activities can be a challenge, but most people have more free time than they like to admit. If you are a student, you probably don't have much choice other than to work out in the evenings or on weekends. If you have a full-time job, your only choice is to train when you're not working. If you are a shift worker, you need to find a martial arts school that has day and evening classes that don't conflict with your work shifts. Some cities don't have schools with day and evening classes. Most schools hold their classes at night. You may have to train at home by yourself when you are working a shift that conflicts with your martial arts school's schedule. If you are in this situation, see if other students are on the same shift; maybe you can train with them. Who knows—maybe you can talk your instructor into letting you have a key to the school so that you can go in and train when they are not around. In some cases this may not be possible, but it's worth a try.

Another time conflict arises for people who have families and wish to train to compete. A lot of spouses do not like to be left at home with the kids while the other one goes out. The best solution that I've seen is to get the whole family involved at the martial arts school. It doesn't always work, but if a majority of the family gets involved, then martial arts training may be seen as a family activity instead of one person's selfish quest. The same solution can be applied to friends who keep bugging you to ditch your training so that you can hang out. Tell them that you'd love to hang out with them *and* train with them. Invite them to try out a class at your school so that they might see and share your passion. It may turn out to be a different type of outing than they originally intended but still be a fun one that friends can share. Maybe your family and friends won't want to train with you. If that's the case, remember that time away from them spent doing something just for you is very healthy. Do not let anyone make you think that it's wrong to take time out for yourself. But in return, always let others have the same privilege.

Arnold Schwarzenegger was once asked to define the word *champion*. He answered by telling a story: Arnold was just about to compete in a bodybuilding competition that he had spent months preparing for. His mother called him and said his father had just died. She assumed he would drop what he was doing, jump on a plane, and fly straight home from the competition. Most people would have. But Arnold did the exact opposite. He nicely told his mother that if there was a way for him to help his father, he would come home immediately. But because his father was already dead, Arnold could no longer help him, so he would return home after his competition was finished and mourn then. Arnold won his competition and flew back home to mourn his father. By Arnold's definition, a true champion does not allow any obstacles or events around him to interfere with his or her concentration or goal, no matter what the circumstances, even if sticking with it is morally questionable in the eyes of others. You must learn to separate the outside world from your goals and dreams and to remain focused and committed, or you probably will fail to achieve those goals and dreams. There are a lot of distractions out there. Stay on the path!

Comprehensive Conditioning

Once you've committed the time to training, you need to understand that physically and mentally preparing for a competition involves not just sparring practice to improve your techniques but also working to improve your flexibility, strength, quickness, and endurance in the ring.

If you are a beginner in the sport, most of your physical training will be sparring to help you gain experience. Beginners will want to try to spar with partners who have more experience than they do, provided these more advanced partners have good control. Nobody wants to get beat up while trying to learn! By working with more experienced and controlled martial artists, you will be able to study how they move and react to your techniques without worrying about having your head taken off in the process. Beginners are usually just struggling with the concept of having someone throw kicks and punches at them. Developing the ability to evade a charging opponent is the first priority and the initial building block to developing further skills.

If you are an advanced fighter, sparring often is a good rule as well, but advanced conditioning and advanced sparring drills become equally important in developing your skills. (See chapter 8 for more information.)

Conquering Your Fears

The journey that a martial artist must take to become a champion fighter can be quite different emotionally than of players in other sports. In most sports, injuries—sometimes very serious ones—do occur, but the main purpose of other sports is to score a goal, make a touchdown, cross the finish line first, hit a home run, and so forth. The intention in other sports is not to kick or punch your opponent to score points. In other words, when you go out on the field to play, you generally don't think about getting beat up.

For some martial artists, the very thought of fighting another human being impedes their performance. They cannot separate sport fighting from a real fight, which has no rules or referee. A real fight is based on anger, hatred, and lack of control; competitive fighting is all about control. All competitors must resolve this problem so that they do not allow the competition to psych them out before they've stepped into the ring. Just remember that sport karate is not full contact. Think of it as a game of tag. Touch the target areas before your opponent can touch yours. Sounds like a lot more fun, doesn't it? It seems more relaxing than punching and kicking each other in the head. It subtracts the violence from the act and makes it a game. In reality it is only a game. You can quit a game anytime you want. You can't stop a real fight when you want out; you have to finish it if you want out.

Taking Care of Yourself

Committing to training also involves considering the use of professionals other than your martial arts instructor. When engaging in heavy workout routines on a regular basis, you will find that your muscular functioning and energy levels become tapped. Sore muscles and joint problems are very common in most athletes. Physiotherapists, chiropractors, and nutritionists can play an important role in athletic performance and rehabilitation from hard workouts and injuries. A physiotherapist's priority is to heal injured muscles and other soft tissues surrounding the skeletal structure, whereas a chiropractor's main concern is the health of the skeletal structure from the neck to the hip area. In some cases the two professions have similar purposes, but they can be very different with regard to therapy. A nutritionist's job is to improve one's performance and recovery time through a scientifically balanced diet and supplements (vitamins, herbs, minerals, and so forth).

If you are currently experiencing muscle and joint problems, scout out local physiotherapists and chiropractors to see what they have to offer. If you have low energy levels and weight-related problems, seek out a qualified nutritionist. (The person working behind the counter at the local health food store most likely is not a qualified nutritionist.) Always consult a professional and get second opinions before putting anything into your body. Research products on your own as well. Even having a chat with your local pharmacist may be helpful. He or she may have some literature or educational information about supplements that can keep you healthy.

ARE YOU READY TO COMPETE?

Sport karate involves controlled sparring; unlike the conventions of a full-contact match, sport karate rules do not allow knockouts and drawing blood. Whereas a full-contact fighter who wants to survive in the ring is usually looking at 15 to 20 hours of training a week, success in sport karate generally requires less training time.

Once you have committed to the time and the training required to successfully compete in sport karate point tournaments, assess your readiness to compete by asking yourself the following questions:

- Do I mind performing in front of large groups of noisy spectators?
- Do I mind performing in a competitive atmosphere?
- Does it make me nervous to get punched or kicked by a martial artist who is not my friend or a member of my school?
- Am I extremely afraid of getting hurt?
- Do I mind giving up my weekends to go to tournaments?
- Do I mind spending extra time training in preparation for tournaments?
- Do I take defeat poorly?
- Do I have a healthy respect for the rules and safety regulations of a tournament?
- Do I have respect for other competitors, judges, and referees?
- Do I practice mind training three or more days a week?

Answering these questions will allow you to honestly assess what you are willing to do to become a competitor. As you can see, when deciding to seriously compete in martial arts events, you must decide how far you are willing to go and what you want to achieve. One good approach is to set your long-term goals first and then outline the steps (short-term goals) required for you to achieve your long-term goals. For example, if you are a beginning competitor and your long-term goal is to be a national or world champion, it's a good idea to try out small, local competitions where there won't be many big-name competitors. This will help you develop your confidence and become accustomed to sparring in a competition atmosphere without becoming overwhelmed. After you start placing first, second, or third in a few tournaments, try moving up into the medium-sized tournaments such as state or provincial tournaments. When you start placing first, second, or third at that level, try working your way up to national-level or larger tournaments. Then, if you want to compete on a world level, you'll have to place (or qualify) at the national-level tournament.

As you gain more experience in competitions, analyze your fights to see where you are making mistakes and getting scored on. This will help you determine what drills to focus on in your practice sessions to improve your technique and strategies. You may find that you are stronger offensively than defensively (or vice versa). It is up to you (and your coach if you have one) to decide what you need to work on based on your experience. You may find it helpful to have your matches videotaped to analyze where you are making mistakes and to analyze other competitors' techniques and strategies. In chapter 8, I discuss in more detail how to set up a training program to help you achieve your goals.

Selecting Tournaments

Sport karate doesn't have one single governing body that sanctions events and oversees all tournaments. Rather, there are many karate association tournament circuits that anyone can compete in. Some of these tournaments don't have a next level for those who qualify or place in the top three. These competitions may give you experience, but if you are looking at gaining points toward a title such as state champion or national champion, choose tournament circuits that work on a qualification system and have succeeding levels to aspire to—whether that's state or provincial, national, or world-class events. Competing in qualification tournaments helps you gauge where you stand relative to other competitors.

If you are seriously seeking to become a champion in sport karate, you are now familiar with some of the building blocks that will get you there: understanding the commitment, evaluating what you're good at and what you need work on to become an effective competitor, and setting the necessary goals. The chapters to come cover how to determine your fighting style, what techniques can be used and how to drill them, and the advanced strategies of sparring. Good combat science and good attitude are the keys to success in the ring. So good luck, and most of all, have fun and keep learning!

2

Defining and Refining a Style

Now that you have established your sport karate goals, it's time to take a look at your particular fighting style and see how it matches up with different opponents' styles you will experience in a tournament. In this chapter we discuss the important differences between certain types of fighters and point out their competition strengths and weaknesses. It is helpful to know what type of fighting style *you* use so that you are aware of what types of strategies your opponents are likely to use against you. Always being one step ahead of your opponent strategically is a priority. Good tournament fighters always watch the preliminary matches that they are not participating in to assess their competition. The following pages will help you identify and prepare for different fighting styles.

BASIC STANCES

There are two main fighting stances: a *side stance* (figure 2.1a), in which the competitor stands perfectly sideways to the opponent, and a *front stance* (figure 2.1b), in which the competitor stands with his chest facing the opponent. Recognizing variations on those stances will help you predict what your opponent has in store for you.

Competitors who use a forward stance tend to be punchers, and those who use a side stance tend to be kickers. But there are no hard-and-fast rules;

a
b

Figure 2.1 Kickers tend to use the side stance (*a*), while punchers tend to prefer the front stance (*b*).

some masters say you can't punch properly from a side stance, but fighters keep proving that statement to be incorrect. Bill Wallace, for example, fights from a side stance and has excellent punching skills in the ring.

All the techniques you will learn in this book can be easily performed from the side stance. The key to a good side stance is not to use a stance that is more than a shoulder-width-and-a-half apart. If your stance is wider than this, your footwork will suffer and you will be slower than you should be in both offensive and defensive maneuvers. The forward stance, however, can limit your effectiveness with certain techniques. For example, both the turn-back kick and the spinning hook kick become awkward from a forward stance. From a forward stance, when you throw a lead-leg side kick, hook kick, or roundhouse kick, you "telegraph" your intentions to your opponent before you even make the kick—that is, your opponent can pick up on what you are going to do before you do it just by noticing the way you get into position for the kick.

We both prefer and use the side stance for sparring purposes because it works seamlessly with our lead-leg kicking systems. The side stance gives us great defensive advantages and allows us to avoid telegraphing our kicks. The side stance puts our hips in proper position to kick.

In addition to individual fighting stances, there are terms that describe how you and your opponent stand in relation to each other. If both competitors have the same foot forward while facing each other (for example, right side forward versus right side forward), they are in what is called a *closed stance* (figure 2.2a). If the competitors have the opposite feet forward while facing

a

Figure 2.2 Closed stance.

b

Figure 2.2 *(continued)* Open stance.

each other (for example, left side forward versus right side forward) they are in what is called an *open stance* (figure 2.2b).

FOUR FIGHTING STYLES

There are four main fighting styles that you will meet in the dojo or ring. It is important to understand what type of fighter you are as well as to size up what type of fighter your competitor is. Experience with different styles will help you determine which tactics to use to score points.

Generally you won't choose what type of fighter you will be; rather you will realize your strengths and fighting type after hours of sparring practice.

Bill Wallace is most well known for his amazing combination attacks with his feet, but he's also an incredible counter- and defensive fighter. The Superfoot System is a fighting method that combines offensive and defensive fighting techniques seamlessly. It is an advanced yet simple to understand method of fighting based on primarily using the lead hand and lead foot for offensive and defensive tactics. It has a very deceptive kicking system which uses a kicking style created by Bill Wallace.

Bill Wallace created his lead-leg kicking system in response to a severe knee injury he sustained in Judo. He puts his strong leg forward and keeps his injured leg back in his side fighting stance. He uses his injured leg as the support leg while kicking. Because he uses his forward leg only for kicking, he therefore does not put undue pressure on his injured knee joint. At first other martial artists thought his method was incorrect and was suicide. It was quite different than the traditional methods of fighting commonly used in the 1960s and 1970s. As his successes grew and very few competitors were able to deal with his techniques, it was surmised that his "weakness" had become a strategic advantage in combat. The lead hand and foot are closer to your opponent, therefore you can strike your opponent faster than with conventional rear hand and foot techniques. The most famous martial artist of all time had used these exact fighting concepts before his untimely death: His name was Bruce Lee.

Aggressive Competitor

The aggressive attacker is usually the opponent who makes the first move or starts most of the engagements during a bout. This type of competitor often uses combination attacks to overpower and off-balance opponents. A good aggressive competitor knows how to use combinations to set up the opponent and score.

Aggressive competitors (sometimes known as pressure fighters) typically make the first move during a match, but their main tactic is to keep kicking and punching, not giving their opponents time to breathe or retaliate. They move forward and do not stop until the end of the round or match. To be a good pressure fighter you must be in top physical condition—with good endurance, strength, and speed—because it is easy to become exhausted while kicking and punching from the start of the round to the end. If you lack stamina, you'll need to build your endurance to become better at this style of fighting.

Defensive Competitor

Defensive (also known as counterattacking) competitors let the opponent make the first move or attack during each engagement so that the opponent will create an opening. Any time you kick or punch, you create an opening on yourself. The defensive competitor's strategy is to take advantage of this momentary weakness. The defensive competitor usually assumes a side fighting stance because this offers fewer targets for the attacking opponent. Defensive fighters want to make the opponent charge forward into them. For example, if the opponent attacks with a backfist, the defensive competitor leans back and sticks a side kick into the opponent's ribs. Defensive competitors are often called counterattacking fighters because they know where all the openings are on the opponent; their response depends on the technique the opponent uses. A defensive fighter is like a spider waiting for an insect to get caught in its web—this type of fighter springs when the opponent is weakest. When you kick you are stuck on one leg and cannot move until you place your foot back on the floor. When you punch you open up your rib cage, head, or midsection. There is no perfect attack. You are always vulnerable somewhere, and this is what the defensive competitor preys on.

Dancer Competitor

Competitors who use the dancer (also known as runner) style are always on the move. They do not stay in one spot for long. By constantly moving, they keep you off balance and distracted. A moving target is more difficult to hit than a stationary one. The moment you fire a kick or punch, dancer competitors are gone. They won't engage in your attack and can be very difficult to counter-attack because they attack from a mobile position rather than a stationary one. In other words, they do not allow you to get set and ready to position yourself to make a counter move. They will hit you as you are trying to follow or line yourself up with them. Boxers Muhammad Ali and "Sugar" Ray Leonard are good examples of fighters with a dancer style. Although both boxers used some aspects of the defensive style as well, their footwork skills put them at the top of boxing. Their ability to dance around their opponents allowed them to evade incoming punches and slip in a counterpunch effortlessly. To be a dancer you must be light on your feet and very energetic. Heavy, awkward, and flat-footed competitors do not make very good dancer competitors.

Footwork and rhythm can be taught to the more uncoordinated fighters, but being a good dancer or runner is usually part of a martial artist's psychological make-up. The best way to deal with runner competitors is to make them chase after you by backing off (thus, reversing their whole strategy) or to corner them with side-to-side movement, faking and feinting until you are close enough to strike. The key is to break their natural rhythm. It's a cat-and-mouse game: The runner is the mouse and the dumb cat does the chasing. Turn yourself into the mouse by not engaging and backing off. I find that this situation is predominant when a much larger opponent spars with a smaller opponent. The bigger fighter does a lot of chasing and missing because the smaller competitor won't engage; the little one runs in fear of being hit by a big monster. If you stop chasing runners from one side of the ring to the other and show them some respect, you can trick them into engaging or attacking so that they'll be in range to kick or punch.

Dragon Competitor

Dragon (or master) competitors can become any type of fighter at will. This means that they have trained extensively in all types of fighting strategies and can fluidly change styles depending on the situation or opponent at hand. They are probably the most dangerous type of fighter because they are flexible in all environments and can change on you instantly, making them difficult to predict. Fortunately, most opponents are usually either more offensive or more defensive. The average practitioner does not spend enough time mastering all the different styles of fighting. Rather, most fighters pick one style that they feel comfortable with and work from there, which is fine—there are many top competitors who are incredibly successful using only one style.

3

Applying the Seven Essential Techniques

One of the most common mistakes martial artists make is thinking that they need hundreds of kicks and punches in their arsenal to be effective in sparring. The truth is that the most effective fighters usually use a handful of the most efficient techniques to claim all their victories. In other words, they think *quality* over *quantity*.

Of course, some argue that if you have fewer techniques, then you have fewer options if things get rough. This is true to a degree but not completely accurate. What you must do is pick a few kicks and punches that cover all four of the main trajectories—the path a kick or punch follows from the chamber position to the intended target.

The following are the four trajectories you want to cover:

1. Straight-line techniques such as the jab punch, reverse punch, front kick, side kick, and turn-back kick

2. Arcing and hooking techniques such as the backfist, ridgehand strike, roundhouse kick, hook kick, and spinning hook kick

3. Over-the-top or downward techniques such as the backfist and axe kick

4. Techniques that come from underneath, such as the undercut punch, side kick, turn-back kick, and front kick (if the target area is the groin)

As you can see from the list, some kicks or punches, depending on your specific body position when you throw them, can be a combination of the four trajectory techniques. Within these four trajectories are seven essential techniques that will take you through any sport karate tournament—the backfist, reverse punch, undercut punch, ridgehand strike, roundhouse kick, side kick, and hook kick. In this chapter we'll take you through each technique.

BACKFIST

The backfist is the most popular hand technique in sport karate competitions because of its simplicity and speed. Anyone can learn how to attack with a backfist, even in the very first day of martial arts training. If you lack flexibility, particularly in your legs, the backfist is a weapon that will help you become a top competitor in the sport karate arena.

From the fighting stance (whether forward or side stance) your lead hand should start low with your rear hand up to protect your jaw and head (figure *a*). As you step forward, raise your elbow up (keeping your forearm parallel to the floor; figure *b*) and extend your forearm, snapping the wrist into the target, striking with the two knuckles closest to the thumb (figure *c*). Normally the path of the motion of the backfist is horizontal, but it also can be launched from a 45-degree angle coming down on top of the opponent's head (figure *d*). The purpose of using the 45-degree angle punch is to go over

a

b

c

d

your opponent's guards (arms and hands positioned for protection) to avoid getting your technique jammed.

Always keep your shoulders loose so that you can snap your backfist out like a whip. This greatly increases your hand speed and reaction time.

Offensive Tactics

Here are two offensive backfist tactics that may work well for you. From a closed fighting stance, slide your rear foot up to your front foot (figures *a* and *b*). Raise your knee to chamber position, execute a lead-leg roundhouse kick at belt level to entice your opponent to lower the guards to protect the abdomen (figure *c*), and deliver a lead backfist to the opponent's head (figure *d*).

a

b

c

d

From a closed fighting stance (figure *a*), slide your rear foot up to your front foot (figure *b*) and raise your knee to chamber position, then execute a side kick at belt level to entice your opponent to block or protect the ribs with the lead guard (figure *c*), and deliver a lead backfist to the opponent's head (figure *d*). We use a side kick in this instance because it is illegal in most tournaments to kick or strike the opponent's back, so a lead-leg roundhouse kick to the back is out of the question. In an open fighting stance, the low roundhouse kick to the belly is not possible. The low side kick is used to distract and lower the opponent's guards.

a

b

c

d

Defensive Tactics

Here are three tactics for defending against a backfist from a closed stance. As the opponent attacks with the backfist, step back about 6 to 12 inches with your rear foot and lean back (figures *a* and *b*) to allow yourself enough space to raise your knee to chamber position without getting jammed, and execute a side kick to the opponent's rib cage (figure *c*). Or, instead of executing a side kick, execute a lead-leg roundhouse kick to the opponent's head if the rear hand is not obstructing the path (figure *d*), or execute a lead-leg hook kick, wrapping it around the opponent's backfist (figure *e*).

These defensive tactics may be executed just as easily in an open stance. An exception, however, is the lead-leg roundhouse to the head, in which your kick would get jammed from an open stance (figure *f*) because of the conflicting body positions.

a

b

c

d

e

f

As the opponent attacks with the backfist, another defensive option is to step forward with your front foot and simultaneously raise your forward arm, jamming and deflecting the backfist upward (figures *a* and *b*), and execute an undercut punch to the opponent's rib cage (figure *c*). Sometimes, depending on the range at which you are fighting, it may be necessary to step back to avoid being hit in the head, but remember that stepping backward while blocking can make you a victim of a combination attack setup. So when blocking a technique you might try stepping into it, turning it into a jamming technique to short-circuit the opponent's forward momentum. Jamming is one of the best tactics to prevent being set up by a combination fighter. (To learn more about jamming, see chapters 6 and 7.)

a

b

c

A third option you can use when your opponent attacks with the backfist is to step back with your rear foot while leaning your body backward to avoid being hit (figures *a* and *b*) and execute a lead ridgehand to the opponent's head (figure *c*). The trick to this technique is in the body lean, which allows you to hide your head behind your shoulder to avoid being hit. In other words, take the target away at the last second so that your opponent is totally committed; this allows you to score while your attacker is off balance.

a

b

c

REVERSE PUNCH

The reverse punch is another popular hand technique used in competition. It is not as fast or as sneaky as the backfist, but it does have some strong applications when timed correctly. The bad thing about executing a reverse punch is that it opens up the centerline of your body, exposing your groin, abdomen, and sometimes your face; the backfist opens your rib cage, but because you're sideways you are less of a target. Remember that any technique that uses the rear hand or foot as the striking weapon always opens up more target areas for the opponent.

To execute the reverse punch, start in a side stance (figure *a*). Step forward with your front foot, turning your toes in the direction of the target to open up your hips while pivoting on the ball of your rear foot for extra penetration and power. Then execute the punch with your rear hand to the intended target (figure *b*).

a

b

Remember to keep your lead hand (guard) up to protect the opposite side of your face. Try to hide the front of your face behind the punching arm and hand as you launch it at the opponent.

Offensive Tactics

Here are two offensive tactics you may use with the reverse punch. From a closed fighting stance, slide your rear foot up to your front foot (figures *a* and *b*), raise your knee to chamber position, and execute a lead-leg roundhouse kick at belt level to entice your opponent to lower the guards to protect the abdomen (figure *c*). Then step down, executing a reverse punch with your rear hand to the opponent's head (figure *d*).

a

b

c

d

Alternatively, step forward with your front foot, executing a backfist toward the opponent's head and enticing the defender to raise the guard up high to block (figures *a* and *b*). Then execute a reverse punch to the midsection (figure *c*). This technique can be used when facing an opponent in an open or closed fighting stance.

a

b

c

Defensive Tactics

There are several ways to defend against a reverse punch. In the first, as you stand in an open fighting stance (figure *a*), the opponent attacks with a reverse punch toward your head (figure *b*). You step backward 6 to 12 inches with your rear foot while leaning backward to avoid being hit. You then execute a side kick to the opponent's midsection (figure *c*). Instead of executing a side kick, you could execute a lead-leg roundhouse kick to the opponent's head if the lead guard is not obstructing the path (figure *d*), or execute a lead-leg hook kick, wrapping it around the opponent's reverse punch (figure *e*), or a lead

a

b

c

d

(continued)

27

e

f

g

ridgehand to the opponent's head (figures *f* and *g*). This last technique can be executed from the closed stance as well. Make sure you lean back properly, protecting your face with your lead shoulder and rear hand.

If you are in an open fighting stance (figure *a*) and the opponent attacks with a reverse punch toward your midsection, lean your weight back toward your rear foot and deflect the punch away with a rear palm block (figure *b*). Then shift your weight toward your front foot and execute a lead backfist to the opponent's head (figure *c*).

a

b

c

UNDERCUT PUNCH

The undercut punch is what we like to call the sneaky version of a reverse punch. We say this because if you execute a reverse punch, you have to turn your hips square to your opponent to release the punch, creating openings on yourself and possibly telegraphing your intentions. With the undercut punch you can keep yourself sideways and pop the punch underneath the opponent's guard almost undetected. The only drawback of the undercut punch is that it is designed for low-level attacks, such as to the rib cage and abdomen. It would be difficult to execute it to the face because you would be forced to turn your hips forward. Remember not to confuse the undercut with the uppercut (used in full-contact competition and illegal in point competition, especially to the head). An undercut is a straight-line technique, whereas an uppercut is a scooping technique.

To execute the undercut punch, start from a side stance and step forward with your front foot (figure *a*). Execute a fake backfist, jab, or jamming high

a

block to open up the opponent's rib area or midsection to you (figure *b*). This technique helps you cloak your rear hand to drop it into the proper chamber position for the undercut, in which your palm faces up and is placed across your own midsection for protection. Once you have created the proper opening, pop the undercut into the target with a little snap just as you make contact (figure *c*).

You can easily break an opponent's ribs, or at least knock the wind out of your adversary, if you hit too hard with the undercut, which could get you disqualified for excessive contact or lack of control. Always have control over your technique. In a real-life street situation, by all means feel free to hit as hard as you want because it is an excellent way to stop, drop, and wind an aggressive attacker.

b

c

Offensive Tactics

To use the undercut punch offensively from a closed fighting stance, step forward with your front foot, executing a backfist toward the head to entice your opponent to raise the guard up high for protection (figures *a* and *b*). Then execute an undercut punch to the exposed rib cage (figure *c*). This technique works from the open fighting stance as well, but make sure your first technique, the backfist, cloaks your undercut so that it is not seen. It is not recommended to use the undercut, or any rear-hand technique, without some sort of opening move with the lead hand, because it could leave you in a vulnerable position as in the reverse punch. The lead hand and foot are important in setting up combinations that end with the rear hand or foot. As a good rule of thumb, use a lead-hand or lead-foot technique as the initial move in all combination attacks because it will keep you safer and will be more deceptive.

a

b

c

Another offensive tactic using the undercut from a closed fighting stance is to slide your rear foot up to your front foot (figure *a*), raise your knee to chamber position (figure *b*), and execute a roundhouse kick high toward the head to raise the guards up (figure *c*). Then step forward with your front foot and jam the front arm with your front arm to prevent your opponent from protecting the exposed ribs (figure *d*), and execute an undercut to the ribs (figure *e*). If you do not have the flexibility to kick high to the head with

a

b

c

(continued)

d   *e*

the roundhouse kick, just kick to belt level because it will serve close to the same purpose—to draw the opponent's guards to the other side of the body to expose the rib cage.

Defensive Tactics

There are a few defensive tactics you can use against an undercut. From an open stance (figure *a*), the opponent steps forward and raises the lead hand for distraction. In turn you step back 6 to 12 inches, transferring your weight to your rear foot, and lean backward keeping your lead arm tight against your body for protection (figure *b*). The opponent launches the undercut punch, and you execute a hook kick to the head, wrapping around the attempted punch (figure *c*). Or you execute a side kick to the midsection, intercepting your opponent before the punch is delivered (figure *d*). Both the hook kick and side kick can be executed in the closed fighting stance as well, but remember that your kick must be quick and snappy. When practicing this drill imagine your opponent blitzing at you faster each time, and visualize yourself countering him. Reaction time is important in all defensive drills.

Defensive drills can be practiced in front of a mirror, with moving target pads or even with a partner, provided you use control. Use your imagination; there is always more than one way to practice a drill. Some methods will always be better and safer than others, depending on the techniques involved.

a

b

c

d

RIDGEHAND STRIKE

The ridgehand strike is basically karate's version of boxing's hook punch because it can be used to hook around your opponent's guards or punches. The only other differences are that the ridgehand strike is an open-hand technique and the striking area is on the side of the knuckle closest to the thumb. It seems to be most useful as a defensive weapon, but it can be used effectively as an offensive move as well. Setting up to score with the ridgehand is usually easier if you have a preceding combination or single technique to set it up, as you will see in the "Offensive Tactics" section that follows. This is not a rule, but most martial artists find that they benefit from a more flowing technique when they use the ridgehand in combination for offensive purposes.

From a side stance, start with your forward hand low to protect your rib cage (figure *a*). Step forward with your front foot while simultaneously raising your elbow, chambering it just as you did for the backfist (figure *b*). Drop your front hand down, keeping your elbow in the same position (figure *c*), then arc your hand around in a circular fashion and strike your opponent's head with the ridgehand.

a

b

c

You chamber the ridgehand the same as the backfist, so your opponent will not know what you will throw until you perform the arcing portion of your attack. Your opponent may actually believe that you are going to throw a backfist and may in turn try to defend against a technique that isn't even coming, possibly creating an opening for your ridgehand.

Offensive Tactics

In the following example the ridgehand strike can be used offensively from a closed fighting stance by stepping forward with your front foot and executing a lead backfist toward the opponent's head (figures *a* and *b*), followed by an undercut to the rib cage (figure *c*). Then as your opponent drops the guards to protect (figure *d*), execute a lead ridgehand to the head (figure *e*). This technique may be executed from the open fighting stance as well. To excel at this combination attack, practice blitzing up and down the gym, gradually increasing the speed. Blitzing simply means moving as fast as you can (usually using a combination attack) so your opponent has no time to prepare to counter. Using a mirror or a partner is extremely useful.

a

b

c

d

e

Another offensive technique using the ridgehand from a closed fighting stance (figure *a*) is to slide your rear foot up to your front foot (figure *b*), raise your knee to chamber position, and execute a lead-leg roundhouse kick to the midsection to entice your opponent to lower the guards (figure *c*). Then step down in front and execute a lead ridgehand to the exposed head (figure *d*).

a

b

c

d

Defensive Tactics

You can defend the ridgehand strike from a closed fighting stance (figure *a*). As your opponent steps forward with the rear foot to execute a ridgehand strike with the forward hand, step back with your rear foot and lean back to avoid being hit (figure *b*). Execute a lead-leg side kick to your opponent's midsection (figure *c*) or a roundhouse kick to the head (figure *d*). You can execute this defensive technique from the open stance except for the counter-roundhouse kick. The problem with the counter-roundhouse kick to the head is that it will get jammed under the opponent's arm before it makes contact with the target because of the body positions and mechanics involved. When it comes to counterattacking, the low side kick to the belt usually has the least chance of getting jammed. When in doubt, counter with a side kick, unless of course your opponent is right up against you. The side kick can be your greatest friend at medium and far ranges.

a

b

c

d

Here is a defensive technique to use from an open (figure *a*) or closed fighting stance: When your opponent steps forward with the lead foot and executes a ridgehand with the rear hand, intercept the attack before it is complete and execute a cross-behind backfist to the head (figure *b*).

a

b

ROUNDHOUSE KICK

Because it can be used easily for offensive and defensive purposes, the roundhouse kick is the most widely used kick in all martial arts competitions. The roundhouse kick can be thrown from the front or rear leg; in this book we demonstrate how to score using the front leg, which is much faster because it is closer to the opponent than the rear leg. Remember that covering distance takes time. In the fight, time and distance to the intended target determine victory or defeat. Other variables are involved, but they are all governed by time and distance. In competitive martial arts most people strike with the instep of the foot because it is faster and snappier like a whip, whereas in many traditional karate and taekwondo schools attackers strike with the ball of the foot, just as in a front kick.

To execute the roundhouse kick, start in a side stance with your forward hand low protecting your rib cage (figure *a*). Step forward about 6 to 12 inches with your front foot, slide your rear foot up to your lead foot (pointing the toes of your rear foot 180 degrees in the opposite direction of the target; figure *b*), raise your knee and foot into the kicking chamber position for protection (with your shin parallel to the floor; figure *c*), and snap the instep of your foot into the intended target (figure *d*).

a

b

c

d

Offensive Tactics

Use the roundhouse kick offensively from an open or closed fighting stance (figure *a*) by sliding your rear foot to your front foot, raising your knee to chamber position (figure *b*), and executing a lead-leg roundhouse kick to your opponent's midsection to draw the guards down (figure *c*). Then bring your leg back to chamber position and execute a lead-leg roundhouse kick to the head (figure *d*).

a

b

c

d

Here is another offensive tactic from an open fighting stance (figure *a*): After you raise your knee to chamber position, execute a lead-leg hook kick toward the head to entice your opponent to lean the head back out of range and to raise the guards (figure *b*). Bring your leg back to chamber position and execute a lead-leg roundhouse kick (figures *c and d*).

a

b

c

d

Defensive Tactics

You can effectively defend against the roundhouse kick from a closed fighting stance (no wider than your own shoulder width) in several ways. As your opponent slides the rear foot to the front foot to attempt a lead-leg roundhouse kick (figure *a*), push or execute a slight hop forward off your rear foot and jam your opponent's leg with your shin (figure *b*). While your opponent is off balance, execute a lead ridgehand to the head (figure *c*). To eliminate the possibility of being scored upon, step into the kick as soon as you see your opponent move toward you. If you wait too long, the kick may get through and develop power that could really hurt. Short-circuit the move before it gets dangerous.

a

b

c

As your opponent slides up to execute a lead-leg round-house kick, you can also execute a stopping side kick at belt level (figure *d*). This technique can be executed in the open fighting stance as well. When using the stopping side kick against kicking attacks, remember to keep your stance no wider than your own shoulders or you will likely get jammed. By keeping your supporting leg (rear leg) closer to the opponent, you will have more reach and will spend less time trying to launch your kick

d

because your rear foot is right underneath your hips. Whenever you kick, your hips have to be directly over your supporting leg or you will have no balance, power, or speed.

As you stand in either an open or closed fighting stance and your opponent slides the rear foot to the front foot (figures *a* and *b*), skip back and lean

a

b

(continued)

47

(figure *c*) to avoid the lead-leg roundhouse kick aimed at your head (figure *d*). As the opponent's foot drops, quickly slide your rear foot to your front foot (figure *e)* and execute a lead-leg hook kick to your opponent's head (figures *f* and *g*). The key is to launch your counterattack as soon as you are out of range of attack.

c

d

48

e

f

g

49

SIDE KICK

The side kick is another powerful and functional technique that can be used easily offensively and defensively. Although it is not quite as fast as the round-house kick, it is used more for knocking an opponent backward and for stopping an incoming charge dead. Another good time to use the side kick is when you're not sure whether your opponent is going to counter. It is difficult to counter a low side kick to the midsection, so it is an excellent clearing technique you can use to gauge an opponent's reaction and to create an opening for another technique. Straight-line techniques are generally more difficult to counter than circular or angular ones. Sidestepping, jamming, and blocking can be used to counter a side kick, but because of the physics of the side kick, even top competitors have a difficult time countering it. At most they usually just get out of the way without retaliating. So once again, the side kick is an excellent way to start a match or deal with a counterfighter just sitting there waiting for you to attack.

From a side stance, start with your forward hand low protecting your rib cage. Step forward about 6 to 12 inches with your front foot (figure *a*). Slide your rear foot up to your lead foot (pointing your toes 180 degrees in the opposite direction of the target; figure *b*). Raise your knee and foot into the kicking chamber position for protection and extend your foot out, snapping the heel into the target (figure *c*).

a

b

c

It's safer to strike with the heel than it is to strike with the blade (outside) of the foot because the heel is perfectly aligned with the tibia (shinbone), which provides stability to the heel. If you hit with the sole, blade, or ball of the foot, you risk injuring your ankle on heavy and sturdy opponents. Your ankle will be forced into bending backward toward you, going past its normal range of motion and causing trauma to the ankle joint. Kicking with the heel is based on the same concept as punching with the two knuckles closest to the thumb; the two knuckles are aligned directly with the bone in the forearm.

Offensive Tactics

From a closed or open fighting stance (figure *a*), an effective offensive tactic is to step forward with your front foot and execute a lead backfist toward the head. This entices your opponent to raise the guards (figure *b*). Slide your rear foot up to your front foot and execute a lead side kick to your opponent's exposed rib cage or midsection (figure *c*).

a

b

c

Another good offensive tactic from a closed or open fighting stance is to slide your rear foot up to your front foot (figures *a* and *b*) and execute a quick lead-leg hook kick toward the head, enticing your opponent to raise the guards (figure *c*). Then quickly return to your start position and execute another quick lead-leg hook kick toward the head and move quickly back to your start position. Now quickly step forward with your front foot, slide your rear foot to your front foot (figure *d*), and execute a lead-leg side kick to the opponent's rib cage or belt level (figure *e*).

Remember that the goal of the two quick hook kicks is to draw your opponent's guards up so that you can set up for the low side kick. You return to your start position for the first two hook kicks so that the defender thinks there is no reason to retreat or back up very far, if at all. Your opponent may feel comfortable enough to simply lean the head out of range to avoid the first two hook kicks; this will program the defender into believing that the

a

b

c

(continued)

d

e

f

next time you kick there is no need to run for the hills. Your opponent will believe that you're going to fall short; that's exactly the impression you want to create when you execute your step, slide, and side kick. Mentally prepare the defender with kicks that always end short; then when your rival is confident or programmed, launch the real technique that goes deep. Usually about two short (or probing) kicks will do for the setup, but all opponents are different. Some may require only one short kick, or two, or even three to be programmed correctly. Experiment in your sparring classes.

You can also perform the offensive tactic effectively by executing one or more quick lead-leg roundhouse kicks toward the head (figure *f*). Return to the start position after each kick before quickly stepping forward with your front foot, sliding your rear foot to your front foot and executing a lead-leg side kick to the opponent's rib cage or belt level.

Just as in the previous example, the two initial probing roundhouse kicks set up your opponent to allow you to score with the side kick without worrying that she'll try to run away. If an opponent has fast reaction time and can move out of range quickly, the probing kicks may be your best bet if you wish to score. The roundhouse kick, side kick, and hook kick can all be used as probing kicks. The jab and backfist can be used for the same purpose as the probing kicks. A well-trained boxer uses the jab constantly to set up an opponent for the finishing or scoring punch.

Defensive Tactics

Defend against the side kick from a closed fighting stance (figure *a*) with feet no wider than your own shoulder width or from an open stance. As your opponent slides up to execute a lead-leg side kick, (figure *b*), execute a stop-

ping side kick to belt level before the incoming kick is finished (figure *c*). Keep your stance no wider than your own shoulders, or you will more than likely get jammed. By keeping your supporting leg (rear leg) close to your opponent, you will have more reach and will spend less time trying to launch your kick because your rear foot is right underneath your hips. Again, whenever you kick, your hips must be directly over your supporting leg or you will have no balance, power, or speed.

a

b

c

Another technique is to intercept as the opponent slides the rear foot to the front foot, before the technique is completed, then execute a cross-behind backfist to the head (figures *a* and *b*).

a   *b*

As soon as you see your opponent move forward, that's when you launch your counterattack. If you wait too long you'll get a side kick in the ribs. This technique relies heavily on exact timing to keep you safe when executing it, so practice hundreds of times from each side before you actually attempt it in real sparring. Some techniques can be dangerous in a real situation until you've really practiced them hard. Through hard practice will come a full understanding of what is required to make them work efficiently and safely. Using a partner is the best way of developing timing for techniques of this sort. Just make sure everyone is wearing proper protection to avoid injuries during training.

HOOK KICK

The hook kick is just what it sounds like. It is a weapon designed to hook around an opponent's guards, punches, and kicks. It is generally thrown at the head of your opponent. You can throw it to the body, but be warned that it can put you in a bad position when it's thrown low because it usually bounces off your opponent's body and may even spin you backward. This puts your back to your opponent, which is usually very bad. If you have the flexibility, our advice is to keep it high because it is much safer strategically.

Another caution with the hook kick is that it is much more difficult to master and control than the roundhouse kick and side kick because of the way it is thrown. It is easy to overshoot your hook kick and become open.

To develop proper balance, always practice your kicks by returning to the same chamber position from which you started. Through proper form and execution you will learn to deliver your techniques safely and with less fear of being countered.

From a side stance, start with your forward hand low protecting your rib cage (figure *a*). Step forward about 6 to 12 inches with your front foot. Slide your rear foot up to your lead foot (pointing your toes 180 degrees in the opposite direction of the target; figure *b*), and raise your knee and foot into the kicking chamber position for protection. The striking area of the foot can be the back of the heel (for power) or the sole of the foot (for reach, figure *c*).

a

b

c

Offensive Tactics

Use the hook kick offensively from a closed fighting stance by sliding your rear foot up to your front foot (figure *a*). Execute a quick lead-leg roundhouse kick toward the head, enticing your opponent to lower the guards (figure *b*). Return quickly to your start position. Execute another quick lead-leg roundhouse kick toward the head and return quickly to your start position. Then quickly step forward with your front foot (figure *c*), slide your rear foot to your front foot, and execute a lead-leg hook kick to the head (figure *d*).

a

b

c

d

From an open fighting stance, slide your rear foot to your front foot (figure *a*), raise your knee to chamber position, and execute a lead-leg side kick toward the belt area to entice your opponent to lower the guards (figure *b*). Bring your leg back to chamber position (figure *c*) and execute a lead-leg hook kick to the head (figure *d*).

If your opponent retreats out of range when you try to execute this combination, try firing a couple probing side kicks first; when there is no attempt to run away anymore, execute the combination. Program your opponent to feel safe!

a

b

c

d

Also from an open fighting stance you can step forward with your front foot and execute a quick jab toward the midsection several times to entice your opponent to draw the guards down (figures *a*, *b*, and *c*). Each time return to your starting position until you quickly step forward with your front foot, and slide your rear foot to your front foot and execute a lead-leg hook kick to the head (figure *d*).

a

b

c

d

Defensive Tactics

Defending effectively against the hook kick is similar to defending against the side kick. From either an open or closed fighting stance (no wider than your own shoulders), as the opponent slides up to execute a lead-leg side kick (figure *a*), execute a stopping side kick to belt level before the incoming kick is finished (figure *b*). Keep in mind that whenever you kick, your hips must be directly over your supporting leg or you will have no balance, power, or speed.

a

b

If you try to step into your opponent's kick at a far range, you might wind up eating it. So be careful. If the attacker is too far away to hit you, it does not make any sense to try to jam the strike. Try to jam a technique only if it has the potential to become dangerous. Jamming is excellent when your opponent is moving in hard and there is little time to react with an immediate kick or punch. You can actually use a jam to buy time or position yourself for your next technique.

From an open or closed fighting stance, as the opponent executes the hook kick, skip back out of range while leaning your head back (figures *a*, *b*, and *c*). As the opponent's foot drops, quickly step forward with your front foot, slide your rear foot to your front foot (figure *d*), and execute a lead-leg hook kick to the head (figure *e*). Remember that the footwork has to be done fast, or your opponent may regain balance and skip back out of the way, just as you did, and then return the favor.

a

b

c

d

e

If you are fighting at a medium to close range and the opponent slides the rear foot to the front foot (figures *a* and *b*) to attempt the hook kick (figure *c*), step forward with your front foot and raise your guards up to jam the kick (figure *d*). Then execute a reverse punch to the head or a lead ridgehand to the head (figures *e* and *f*).

a

b

(continued)

63

c

d

e

f

4

Manipulating the Opponent by Drawing and Luring

There are several ways you can control the action by luring your opponent into your counterattack. In this chapter we focus on ways you can use drawing and luring tactics to help you score. These tactics are especially effective when you face an opponent who forces you to make the first move. For example, a defensive fighter or an opponent who is physically exhausted or scared is unlikely to throw anything until it's absolutely necessary. In essence the following drills are designed to entice your opponent to engage (or counterattack). This then allows *you* to counter your opponent's counterattack. You are literally setting a trap for your opponent, hoping he will walk right into it.

DRAWING

Drawing, or luring, is the art of encouraging a counterattack in order to position your opponent for your counterattack. By drawing, you create an obvious opening that lures your opponent to attack what is perceived as an easy score. For this reason, an otherwise uncommitted counterfighter (who typically waits for you to make the first move) is willing to initiate an attack, providing you with the opportunity to counterattack. Even more important, you already know where this attack is aimed, so you can prepare the perfect counter, increasing your chances of success.

The ideal situation in which to use the drawing concept is when facing a counterfighter who never attacks. If you are a counterfighter, how can you execute a counterattack if your opponent just stands there and looks at you? When two counterfighters face each other, often both stand in hard fighting stances waiting for the other one to attack. If no one attacks, then there isn't a fight and no points are scored.

So how do you entice someone to counterattack? A fighter counterattacks for one main reason: The counterattacker sees a threatening kick or punch coming and, out of necessity, simply defends against it. So now that you know that you have to attack to draw the opponent into counterattacking, how do you do so without getting countered yourself?

Drilling scenarios prepare you for what you will meet in the competition arena. Speed in your initial technique is crucial for success. If you are too slow your opponent will have too much time to react and think. Your opponent may counter you before you can finish setting up your trap. Your initial drawing techniques should be like a whipping action—quick, short, and snappy. Do not try to chase after your opponent. Your only goal for your initial technique is to make your opponent feel uncomfortable and to produce a retaliatory technique that you are ready to counter. Quick footwork also ensures that you safely return to your start position after your drawing and luring techniques so that you're ready to counterattack your opponent's retaliation.

It's also important to make sure your drawing techniques feel like a real threat to your opponent. For example, if you throw a backfist at the head and your opponent doesn't react to it by at least leaning back or putting the guards up, you probably are not close enough. And if there is no reaction to your initial drawing technique, the rest of your strategy will probably fail. A counterfighter must feel threatened to counterattack accordingly.

When practicing drawing drills with a partner, sometimes allow your partner to spontaneously choose a counterattack so that you can develop better reaction time and problem-solving skills. This way you can still isolate the drawing concept you are working on, and you can start to see how an opponent may react to the initial technique you throw out there. The way you throw your initial drawing technique—high, low, straight in, or arcing—will greatly affect how your opponent chooses to retaliate.

You can also experiment with having your partner start in different types of fighting stances, facing you in a boxer-style stance or assuming a perfect side stance. Depending on the stance being used, certain techniques will be more comfortable than others when it is your partner's turn to retaliate. The choice of an open or closed stance also will affect the decision-making process.

Working with different types of partners when doing these drills can be beneficial. Body type—tall, short, light, heavy, and so forth—is another variable to fool around with. All people move differently. When sparring, find your opponent's rhythm—the unique way of moving and preferred tempo of that fighter. Unfortunately, there is no real secret to learning how to figure out someone's tempo. It is developed through regular sparring with different types of opponents and constant practice of sparring drills.

The following drills are scenarios to help you train yourself to lure your opponent into counterattacking. The trick is to learn how to throw your kicks and punches so that it is difficult for your opponent to counter them.

1. From a closed fighting stance, slide your rear foot up to your front foot (figures *a* and *b*).

2. Execute a lead-leg roundhouse kick toward the midsection, causing your opponent to protect the area (figure *c*).

3. Drop your kicking foot down right beside your support leg. If you don't place your foot right beside your support leg, your opponent will have the opportunity to counter. When your feet are right beside each other, all you have to do is lean back and kick.

a

b

4. As your opponent decides to counter with a reverse to your head, lean back to avoid the punch (figure *d*).

5. Execute a hook kick to your opponent's head (figure *e*).

If you step forward after your lead-leg roundhouse, you are almost flat-footed, and if you want to kick from there, you have to take the time to shift all your body weight back to your rear foot and then lean back and try to kick. By this time your opponent will have already counterpunched you in the head.

c

d

e

1. From a closed fighting stance slide your rear foot up to your front foot (figure *a*).
2. Execute a lead-leg roundhouse kick toward the head. The opponent leans the head slightly out of range (figure *b*).
3. Drop your kicking foot down right beside your support leg (figure *c*).
4. The opponent decides to counter with a backfist to your head. Lean back to avoid the punch and execute a hook kick to your opponent's head (figure *d*) or a side kick to the ribs (figure *e*).

You can also try this drill with the opponent deciding to counter with a rear-leg roundhouse kick to your midsection. You immediately execute a side kick to the opponent's head or midsection, intercepting the roundhouse kick before its completion.

The key is always to be one step ahead of your opponent. Knowing how your opponent will retaliate to your movements can create openings that weren't there a second ago. Use your first kick or punch as bait to draw your opponent into a trap. Remember that sparring is just like playing chess. You cannot win the game in the first move alone. You sometimes have to see what makes your opponent tick by throwing things out there to see what the reaction will be. After that, it's up to you how you use that information.

a

b

c

d

e

71

1. From a closed fighting stance, slide your rear foot up to your front foot and execute a very quick, probing lead-leg roundhouse kick toward the midsection (figures *a*, *b*, and *c*).

2. As your opponent protects the area, quickly return to your start position (figure *d*).

a

b

c

d

3. As your opponent decides to counter with a backfist to your head, lean back to avoid the punch, and execute a lead-leg roundhouse kick to your opponent's head (figures *e* and *f*).

This technique is excellent if you think that your opponent is going to be right on top of you after you throw your first kick. You want to be in and out of range and ready to counter the retaliation.

e

f

1. From an open fighting stance slide your rear foot up to your front foot and execute a very quick, probing lead-leg side kick toward your opponent's midsection (figures *a*, *b*, and *c*).

2. As the opponent leans back and protects the area, quickly return to your start position (figure *d*).

a

b

3. The opponent decides to counter with a reverse punch to your head (figure *e*).

4. Lean back to avoid the punch, and execute a lead ridgehand strike to your opponent's head (figure *f*).

c

d

e

f

1. From a closed fighting stance (with your feet about a shoulder-width apart), step forward with your front foot and execute a probing lead backfist toward your opponent's head (figures *a* and *b*).

2. As your opponent leans back to avoid being hit, quickly return to the original start position.

3. Step forward and execute another probing lead backfist toward the head and quickly return to your start position as your opponent leans back to avoid being hit.

a

b

4. Your opponent decides to counter with a backfist (figure c).
5. Lean back and execute a lead-leg side kick to the rib cage (figure d).

You can also counter with a hook kick or lead-leg roundhouse kick to the head, depending on where your opponent's guards are at the time. Always try to counterattack the unprotected target areas. In other words, if one side of the head is protected, just kick it on the other side. You also can do the hook kick countering technique in an open fighting stance, but not the lead-leg roundhouse kick because it will get jammed underneath your opponent's attacking arm.

c

d

1. From a closed or open fighting stance, slide your rear foot up to your front foot, and execute a probing lead-leg side kick (figures *a*, *b*, and *c*) or a roundhouse kick toward the head.

2. As your opponent reacts by leaning the head slightly out of range, return to your start position (figure *d*).

3. As your opponent decides to counter with a turn-back kick to your midsection, immediately take a quick step backward to evade the kick (figure *e*).

4. As your opponent drops the foot toward the floor, explode forward by stepping with your lead foot (figure *f*).

a

b

c

d

5. Slide your rear foot up to your front foot and execute a hook kick to the head (figures *g*, *h*, and *i*). You can also counter with a lead-leg roundhouse kick to your opponent's head, depending on where the guards are at the time.

e

f

g

h

i

FAKE KICKING

Fake kicks are kicks that don't actually get finished. You can also think of them as half kicks because they start the same way as real kicks except they don't actually make the final extension. They are specifically designed to make an opponent think that a certain kick has been launched but, in midstream, it turns into a completely different kick. Fake kicks are another method used to entice your opponent into reacting defensively. We discuss three fake kicks that you can use with great success after much diligent practice. You'll need to spend a lot of time experimenting with these kicks while sparring in order to use them effectively in competition. You will find that the stance you use (open or closed) will affect how your opponent reacts to your fake kick. In the following drills we present examples showing how to use fake kicks to create openings on your opponent.

1. Face your opponent in an open or closed fighting stance (figure *a*).
2. Raise your knee up into a side kick chamber position (with the heel targeted at the belt level) to draw your opponent's guards down low (figures *b* and *c*).
3. Execute a lead backfist to your opponent's exposed head (figure *d*).

a

b

c

d

1. Face your opponent in an open or closed fighting stance (figure *a*).

2. Raise your knee up into a side kick chamber position (with the heel targeted at the belt level) to draw your opponent's guard down low (figures *b* and *c*).

3. Retract your leg to chamber position without lowering it to the floor (figure *d*).

4. Execute a roundhouse kick to the opponent's exposed head (figure *e*). You can also use a hook kick instead of the roundhouse kick if the opponent has placed a guard in the way.

a

b

c

d

e

83

1. Face your opponent in an open or closed fighting stance and slide your rear foot toward your front foot (figures *a* and *b*).

2. Raise your knee up into a roundhouse kick chamber position (with the instep of the foot targeted at the belly) to draw your opponent's guard down low to protect the abdomen (figure *c*).

3. Execute a hook kick to your opponent's exposed head (figures *d* and *e*).

a

b

c

d

e

Basically you are throwing a hook kick from a roundhouse kick chamber position to make your opponent think that a roundhouse kick is coming. You just switch into the hook kick when your opponent reacts, creating an opening on the other side of the head.

1. Face your opponent in an open or closed fighting stance (figure *a*).
2. Raise your knee up into a roundhouse kick chamber position (with the instep of the foot targeted at the belly) to draw your opponent's guard down low to protect the abdomen (figures *b* and *c*).
3. Execute a roundhouse kick to the exposed head (figure *d*).

a

b

c

d

The key in this technique is to make sure that your fake roundhouse kick low to the belly actually looks as if its only target is the belly. Try to aim the instep at the belt and no higher to ensure that your opponent reacts properly. If you aim your fake kick at the solar plexus (chest), you will allow your opponent enough time to put the guards back up to protect the face.

Fake Hook Kick Into a Roundhouse Kick

1. Face your opponent in an open or closed fighting stance (figure *a*).
2. Raise your knee up into a hook kick chamber position (do this by raising your foot at an approximate 45-degree angle to your opponent) to draw your opponent's guards and attention to that side of the body (figures *b* and *c*).

a

b

c

3. Bring the knee back to chamber position, then execute a roundhouse kick to the exposed head (or belly if you are in a closed stance; figures *d* and *e*).

The fake hook kick is an excellent way to disrupt an opponent's rhythm. It looks as though a kick is on its way to a target, but the great thing is that your opponent doesn't even need to figure out what type of kick it is. The defender reacts to seeing a leg fly out from the side and thinks, *Whoa! What's that? I better cover up on that side or move in the opposite direction.* By moving in the opposite direction, your opponent walks directly into your roundhouse kick. This technique is a Bill "Superfoot" Wallace favorite and trademark technique.

d

e

Fake Hook Kick Into a Side Kick

1. Face your opponent in an open or closed fighting stance (figure *a*).
2. Raise your knee up into a hook kick chamber position (do this by raising your foot at an approximate 45-degree angle to your opponent) to draw your opponent's guards and attention to that side of the body (figures *b* and *c*).
3. Execute a side kick to the exposed ribs or belly (figures *d* and *e*).

a

b

c

d

e

Remember that the fake hook kick is the exact opposite of the fake round-house kick. So the way your opponent reacts to fakes and whether you are facing each other in an open or closed stance will greatly influence which fake kick (roundhouse or hook kick) will work best in that situation. This does not necessarily mean that you can't use either one; you just may find that certain opponents react better to certain fake kicks. The key once again is to experiment with both and see what happens. You may be surprised at what makes your opponent react and what doesn't. Fighters will react differently. Trial and error is a fundamental aspect of life and combat.

Programming Your Opponent for a Fake

It is not always necessary but can sometimes be a good a idea to throw a real kick first to ensure an opponent is properly programmed to react to your fake kick. For example, if you choose to use a fake hook kick to set up for a scoring roundhouse kick, follow these steps:

1. First throw a real hook kick very fast toward the head, forcing your opponent to react out of fear of being hit. This sets up a defensive response to your next move.

2. Now execute the fake hook kick, making it look as similar as possible to the first kick before you refold your knee halfway through to prepare for a roundhouse kick. This is the main bait to lure your opponent into creating an opening.

3. With your knee now chambered in the roundhouse kick position, snap a roundhouse kick into the head. Here is where you score.

Some opponents are too well trained to get hit by a simple direct attack. Disguising the intended technique is necessary against advanced competitors. The order in which you execute your techniques is important and can vary with different opponents. Experimenting during sparring practice is a key factor in developing your fake kicking skills.

How well you control your opponents is based on how well you can control their reactions to your initial techniques. Drawing and faking are two ways that you can safely launch probing kicks to check and test your opponent's reactions. Because they are designed to get you in and out of range fast, drawing and faking give you the time and distance to counter your opponent's retaliation without being scored on. Remember, as with anything, you need to repeatedly practice these techniques in drills to master them. Once you understand the concept of drawing and faking, you can start to develop your own drills and strategies to more comfortably fit your fighting style.

5

Defending
and Countering
Kick Combinations

When you're defending against kick combinations, the best thing you can do is not let the combination even get started. In other words, counter, or jam, your opponent's first kick. If you allow that first or second kick to come out, your opponent can develop more forward momentum and become more powerful, faster, and dangerous. Remember that a combination attack is designed to set up an opponent for the last technique, the "killer." So if you disarm your opponent on the first kick, you will never have to deal with the killer technique.

As a martial artist, however, you must always prepare yourself for the worst-case scenario. What if you react too slowly or there is not enough time to counter or jam the first kick? You have three other choices:

1. Back up with defensive footwork.
2. Side step.
3. Perform a combination of the two.

USING DEFENSIVE FOOTWORK

Any serious competitor must understand how to use defensive footwork against kicking techniques. Footwork, when combined with kicking and punching, will determine the outcome of all engagements. Proper and well-timed footwork is what puts you in position to evade and score. Poor footwork, on the other hand, is what positions you to be scored on, thus ruining your counterattack. The two most important and basic pieces of footwork, which all other advanced footwork is based on, are the push step (backward) and the quick retreat. When you can make these two pieces of footwork flow effortlessly, you will notice that your sparring will greatly improve.

Perform the push step (backward) by standing with your feet about shoulder-width apart in side stance (figure 5.1a). Then push off your front foot and step backward with your rear foot (figure 5.1b); trail your front foot with you and return to a balanced fighting stance (figure 5.1c).

a   *b*

c

Figure 5.1   The push step (backward) allows you to quickly avoid an opponent's strikes.

In the quick retreat, stand with your feet about two shoulder-widths apart in a side fighting stance (figure 5.2*a*). Draw your front foot to your rear foot (figure 5.2*b*); as your front foot almost touches your rear foot, step back with your rear foot and return to a balanced fighting stance (figure 5.2*c*).

a   *b*

c

Figure 5.2 The quick retreat provides a way to move away from your opponent and then back in for your own countermove.

When you have mastered the footwork techniques separately, you can then combine them, starting with the backward push step followed by the quick-retreat footwork. Together, these two pieces of footwork are especially effective when a charging opponent covers a lot of distance or attacks deep. Sometimes if an opponent is coming in really deep, you might use one backward push step followed by the quick-retreat footwork two to three times just to get out of range of the attack or combination.

In dealing with a strong combination kicker, learning the art of sidestepping can be beneficial. Combination attacks are designed to be launched in a straight line to back the opponent up in a straight line. If you sidestep the first or second technique, your opponent's momentum is immediately short-circuited because you are no longer in the line of fire. Be a matador let the charging bull come at you as you lure him into believing that his target will be there when he arrives. At the last split second, remove the target from his reach. The same concept can be used against a charging puncher. Practice the drills in this chapter and you will develop the footwork skills needed to sidestep the charging combination kicker.

DEFENDING AGAINST SINGLE KICKS

Developing a strong stopping side kick will give you an edge when facing other kickers. There is nothing more frustrating than getting a counter-side kick in your ribs or midsection every time you try to kick. Standing with your feet no more than shoulder-width apart ensures that you won't get jammed as you lift your leg to counterkick. As soon as you see any forward movement, stick that side kick straight out into the attacker's body. Strike with your heel for power and to protect your ankle.

Jamming your opponent is also an ideal method for short-circuiting kick attacks. To learn how to use jamming to stop an opponent's attack before it gets dangerous, see chapter 7.

Countering the Roundhouse Kick

Practice the following drills to neutralize your opponent's roundhouse kick.

1. Stand in a closed fighting stance with feet no wider than shoulder-width apart (figure *a*). Your opponent slides the rear foot to the front (figure *b*) to attempt a lead-leg roundhouse kick.

a

b

2. Step forward with your front foot into the incoming kick and jam the leg by using your forearms (figure *c*).

3. While your opponent is still off balance, execute a lead ridgehand to the head (figure *d*). It is important that you step into the kick as soon as you see a move toward you to eliminate the possibility of a score by your opponent. If you wait too long, the kick may get through and develop power that could really hurt. Short-circuit the move before it gets dangerous.

c

d

1. Stand in a closed or open fighting stance with feet no wider than shoulder-width apart (figure *a*). Your opponent slides the rear foot to the front (figure *b*) to attempt a lead-leg roundhouse kick.

2. Step forward with your front foot into the incoming kick and jam the leg by using your forearms (figure *c*).

3. Before your opponent can regain full balance or finish the kick, execute a stopping side kick at belt level (figures *d* and *e*).

a

b

c

d

e

When using the stopping side kick against kicking attacks, remember to keep your stance no wider than your own shoulder width, or you will likely get jammed. By keeping your supporting leg (rear leg) closer to your opponent, you will have more reach and will spend less time trying to launch your kick because your rear foot is right underneath your hips. As we've emphasized before, whenever you kick, your hips must be directly over your supporting leg or you will have no balance, power, or speed.

Hook Kick Defense

1. Stand in either a closed or an open fighting stance (figure *a*).
2. As the opponent slides the rear foot to the front foot (figure *b*), skip back and lean to avoid the lead-leg roundhouse kick aimed at your head (figure *c*).

a

b

c

3. As your opponent's foot drops, quickly slide your rear foot to your front foot (figure *d*).

4. Execute a lead-leg hook kick to the head (figure *e*). The key is to launch your counterattack as soon as you are out of range of your opponent's attack.

d

e

Countering the Side Kick

In addition to the stopping side kick defense (see pages 100-101), the following is another good way to shut down a side kick. Using a partner is the best way to develop timing for techniques of this sort of counterattack. Just make

Cross-Behind Backfist Defense

1. Stand in an open or closed fighting stance (figure *a*).
2. Your opponent slides the rear foot to the front foot (figure *b*).

a

b

sure both you and your partner are wearing proper protection to avoid injuries during training. Proper protection includes head gear and gloves as well as groin, foot, and shin protectors, all of which should be available for use at your martial arts gym.

3. Before the attacker can complete this technique, intercept the strike and execute a cross-behind backfist to the head (figure c).

c

Remember, as soon as you see forward movement, that's when you launch your counterattack. If you wait too long you wind up getting a side kick in the ribs. This technique relies heavily on exact timing for safety, so practice hundreds of times on each side before you attempt this move in real sparring. Some techniques can be dangerous in a real situation until you've practiced them to mastery; through hard practice you will come to a full understanding of what is actually required to make them work efficiently and safely.

Countering the Hook Kick

In addition to a stopping side kick (see pages 100-101), here are two other good ways to counter an opponent's hook kick.

Hook Kick Defense

1. Stand in a closed fighting stance (also works from an open stance) (figure *a*).
2. Your opponent slides the rear foot to the front foot and attempts a hook kick (figures *b* and *c*).

a

b

c

Remember that footwork that involves stepping forward and sliding up has to be done fast; otherwise your opponent can regain balance and skip back out of the way, just as you did, and then return the favor.

3. Skip back out of range while leaning your head back (see figure c).
4. As your opponent's foot starts to drop, quickly step forward with your front foot (figure d), slide your rear foot to your front foot (figure e), and execute a lead-leg hook kick to the head (figure f).

d

e

f

1. Stand in an open fighting stance at medium to close range from your opponent (figure *a*).

2. Your opponent slides the rear foot to the front foot (figure *b*) and attempts to execute a hook kick.

3. Step forward with your front foot and raise your guards up to jam the incoming kick (figure *c*).

a

b

c

4. Execute a reverse punch to the head (figure *d*) or a lead ridgehand to the head (figure *e*).

d

e

If your try to step into your opponent's kick at a far range, you might wind up eating it. So be careful. If your attacker is too far away to hit you, it does not make any sense for you to try to jam the incoming moves. You only try to jam a technique if it has a potential of becoming dangerous. Jamming is excellent when your opponent is moving in hard and there is very little time to react with an immediate kick or punch. Jamming can actually be used to buy time or position yourself for your next technique.

DEFENDING AGAINST COMBINATION-KICK ATTACKS

You must learn how to defend against single-kick attacks before attempting to learn how to defend against combination-kick attacks. The reason for this is that these two kinds of attacks are directly related, and single attacks are

Countering the Rear-Leg Roundhouse Combination Attack

By starting in a closed stance with feet shoulder-width apart, you can easily step back by pushing off your front foot when you begin your evasive footwork. To step backward with your rear foot really fast, you must first push off of your front foot to get that burst. Just like skating—you have to push off the opposite foot to move forward with the other foot.

1. Stand in a closed fighting stance with your feet about shoulder-width apart (figure a).
2. Your opponent launches a rear-leg roundhouse kick toward you at belt level (figure b).
3. Step back with your rear foot (figure c) and draw your front foot to your rear foot to finish evading the first kick (figure d).
4. As your opponent attempts to execute another rear-leg roundhouse kick (high to your head this time, with the opposite leg), execute a lead-leg side kick to the midsection (figure e).

a

b

easier to learn in the beginning. Because the word combination means more than one, it also means you technically have more to worry about. Don't make things complicated for yourself.

c

d

e

It will take some time for you to coordinate your feet to execute the footwork in this drill, so be patient. Keep practicing until it becomes second nature.

1. Start in an open fighting stance.
2. As your opponent slides the rear foot to the front foot and attempts to finish a side kick, skip back out of range (figures *a* and *b*).
3. As your opponent places the front foot on the floor, draw your front foot to your rear foot.

a

b

4. As your opponent launches a turn-back kick, step with your front foot to your open side (figure *c*).

5. Pivot on your foot about 80 to 90 degrees, letting the turn-back kick fly by you (figure *d*).

6. Step forward with your front foot and execute a backfist to the head (figure *e*).

c

d

e

This drill may feel a little awkward in the beginning because most martial artists struggle in the intricate footwork department. But daily practice will help you develop excellent defensive footwork.

1. Start from an open fighting stance (figure *a*).
2. Your opponent launches a rear-leg roundhouse kick toward you at belt level, and you skip back out of range by drawing your front foot to your rear foot (figure *b*).
3. As your front foot reaches your rear foot, step back with your rear foot to finish evading the first kick (figure *c*).

a

b

c

4. As your opponent turns away from you to attempt a spinning hook kick toward your head, step off the line of fire toward your blind side (figure *d*).
5. Pivot on your foot about 80 to 90 degrees, letting the spinning hook kick fly by you (figure *e*).
6. Step forward with your front foot and execute a backfist to the head (figure *f*).

d

e

f

Keep yourself covered and out of range to avoid being set up to be scored on. Launch your counterbackfist *before* your opponent's foot touches the floor—that is, before your attacker can regain balance.

1. Start from a closed fighting stance.

2. As your opponent slides the rear foot to the front foot and raises the knee to chamber position, step back with your rear foot (figures *a* and *b*).

a

b

3. Lean back out of range, covering your midsection as your opponent executes a lead-leg roundhouse kick (figure *c*).

4. Your opponent returns the leg to chamber position while you continue leaning back out of range (figure *d*).

c

d

(continued)

5. The opponent executes another lead-leg roundhouse kick, toward your head this time (figure *e*).

6. Make sure your rear hand is protecting your face while you continue to lean back.

7. As your opponent drops the foot to the floor, shift your weight forward and execute a lead backfist to the head (figures *f* and *g*).

e

f

g

6

Beating the Opponent's Best Punch

One of the toughest things to deal with in sparring or competing is a blitzing combination puncher. Blitzing is when a fighter charges hard and fast at an opponent with a lightning-fast combination of techniques. Although kicking combinations can be extremely fast, a hand combination can be three to four times as fast. This is because in kicking, at least one foot has to be on the ground before you can launch your next kick (unless you're capable of doing the bicycle kick from the movie *Mortal Kombat*). With punching, however, you can have your second punch on the way just as the first hits its target, and you can run at your opponent simultaneously. So with punches, you're able to cover more distance in a shorter time.

Although the description you just read may make kicking seem inferior to punching, that is not the case. Punching has its advantages over kicking when it comes to speed, but kicking has two main advantages over punching. With a kick, you can be farther away from your target than you can be with a punch. Also, every time you punch you open up your rib cage as a potential target because your arm is attacking rather than acting as a guard. With kicking you can keep your guards positioned to protect your body and head while you strike. You can't protect everything while you fight, but kicking does offer some defensive advantages by allowing you to guard specific areas.

Punching blitzes are extremely difficult to defend against because of the speed factor. A fighter who likes to execute blitzing hand combinations uses the elements of surprise and confusion as a method of overpowering the opponent. The blitzing competitor charges hard and throws as much at the opponent as quickly as humanly possible, figuring that something is bound to get in before the defender has a chance to retaliate.

As we discussed in chapter 5, countering or jamming an opponent on the first technique is the safest and most effective method strategically. Of course, once again we have to prepare for the worst by designing and drilling methods that we can use in case the opponent is in position to get that second or third punch out. Of course, the best way to prepare for the worst is to practice specific drills until they become automatic. This will help you train to handle specific scenarios in a tournament. In addition to practicing various scenarios, keep several guidelines in mind while training.

- Get into the habit of leaning back to avoid being hit. Your partner should always try to hit you in the head as you practice avoiding incoming techniques. If your opponent does not actually try to hit you while you practice your drills, you will develop a false sense of timing and distance that could be disastrous when you use the techniques in actual sparring. To avoid injury, wear lots of padding and use control during your drills.

- When practicing, experiment by having your partner launch the attack from different ranges. Explore and drill from close, medium, and far ranges. The closer your opponent is, the faster you have to lean back and react to avoid being hit. When you are farther away, you have more time to react and usually have more options available to you. At medium and far ranges, counterkicking is much easier because you have more time to chamber your knee. At closer ranges, it is more difficult to chamber the leg without being jammed. However, kicking at close range is not impossible. It is a skill like any other that must be developed through trial and error. Footwork, leaning the body, and chambering the leg properly are the essential components to master in close-range counterkicking.

- Improving your flexibility is an important goal to keep in mind. A karate competitor should stretch 10 to 30 minutes as part of warm-up exercises and 10 to 30 minutes after the training session as a cool-down. It is important for kickers to do specific stretches that develop the adductor and hamstring muscle groups.

- Study the forward movement your opponent uses to execute a hand technique. Notice forward body lean required to reach out to get you. The movements of the shoulders and hips are the keys to detecting what type of technique your opponent will throw. If the lead shoulder comes forward but the body remains more sideways, your opponent probably will throw a technique with the lead hand. If the hips turn square as your opponent moves forward toward you, it means a technique thrown with the rear hand is likely.

In addition to the guidelines mentioned previously, you should know several basic body and arm positions that can be used to defend against blitzes.

Straight-line attack to the head (jab or reverse punch). Lean back out of range of the punch. Keep your chin tucked into your shoulder with your rear hand up for extra protection (figure 6.1*a*).

Straight-line attack to the body (jab or reverse punch). The same defensive concept is used to protect the body as in a straight-line attack to the head. Lean back out of range, keeping your chin tucked into your shoulder with your rear hand up for extra protection. Keep your lead down low to protect your ribs (figure 6.1*b*).

Arcing techniques to the head (backfist in an open stance). Once again, lean back out of range, keeping your chin tucked into your shoulder. Put your rear hand up for extra protection for your face (figure 6.1*c*).

Arcing techniques to the head (backfist in a closed stance). Lean back out of range, keeping your chin tucked into your lead shoulder with your rear hand up for extra protection. Because you are being attacked with the backfist in a closed stance, the key is to use the body lean to avoid your opponent's attack (figure 6.1*d*).

Arcing techniques to the body (ridgehand in a closed stance). Lean back out of range, keeping your chin tucked into your lead shoulder with your rear hand up for extra protection. As with protection against the backfist, use the body lean to avoid your opponent's attack, plus bend your lead arm and pull your fist to your hip to block the attack (figure 6.1*e*).

Arcing techniques to the head (ridgehand in an open stance). Lean back out of range, keeping your chin tucked into your lead shoulder with your rear hand up for extra protection for your face (figure 6.1*f*).

a

b

c

d

Figure 6.1 Advanced body lean defense and hand position.

e *f*

Figure 6.1 *(continued)* Leaning takes the target away from the opponent.

The following scenario drills will help you train yourself to react quickly and effectively to defend punches. A competitor must be able to defend against the backfist, the undercut punch, the reverse punch, and the ridgehand strike as well as combination attacks.

COUNTERING THE BACKFIST

The following three drills will prepare you to defend a backfist. The backfist is very similar to a jab punch in boxing. It is a quick, snappy little punch, generally thrown with the lead hand. The backfist, however, does not travel in a straight-line like the jab punch. Rather, the backfist comes at you from an angle and is extremely fast. Constant repetition of the following drills will develop the skills needed to effectively neutralize the backfist.

1. Stand in a closed fighting stance; your opponent attacks with the backfist (figure a).
2. Step forward with your front foot and simultaneously raise your forward arm, jamming and deflecting the incoming backfist upward (figure *b*).
3. Execute an undercut punch to the rib cage (figure *c*).

Sometimes, depending on the range at which you are fighting, it may be necessary to step back to avoid being hit in the head. But remember that stepping backward while blocking can make you the victim of a combination attack setup. So when blocking a technique, try stepping into it, if possible, and turning it into more of a jamming technique to short-circuit your opponent's forward momentum. Jamming is one of the best tactics to prevent being set up by a combination fighter (see also chapter 7).

a

b

c

1. Stand in an open fighting stance; your opponent attacks with the back-fist.
2. Step back with your rear foot (figure *a*) while leaning your body backward to avoid being hit.
3. Execute a lead ridgehand to the head (figure *b*).

The trick to this technique is in the body lean, which allows you to hide your head behind your shoulder to avoid being hit. In other words, take the target away at the last second when your opponent is totally committed to the punch. This allows you to score while your attacker is off balance.

a

b

1. Stand in a closed fighting stance (figure *a*); your opponent attacks with a backfist.

2. Step back 6 to 12 inches with your rear foot and lean back to allow enough space for you to raise your knee to chamber position without being jammed (figure *b*).

a

b

c

3. Execute a side kick to the rib cage (figure c). Instead of a side kick you could execute a lead-leg roundhouse kick to the head if your opponent's rear hand is not obstructing the path (figure d); or you could go with a lead-leg hook kick, wrapping it around your opponent's backfist (figure e).

d

e

This defensive technique works just as easily from an open stance except for the lead-leg roundhouse to the head option. If you perform that defense from an open stance, your kick will get jammed because of the conflicting body positions.

COUNTERING THE UNDERCUT PUNCH

Here are two great ways to defend against an undercut punch.

Hook Kick Defense

1. Stand in a closed fighting stance; your opponent steps forward and raises the lead hand for distraction.
2. Step back 6 to 12 inches, transferring your weight to your rear foot (figure *a*).
3. Lean backward, keeping your lead arm tight against your body for protection (figure *b*).
4. Your opponent then launches the undercut punch.
5. Execute a hook kick to the head, wrapping around the incoming punch (figure *c*).

   You can execute this technique effectively from an open fighting stance as well, but remember that your kick must be quick and snappy. When practicing this drill, imagine your opponent blitzing at you faster and faster each time, and visualize yourself countering the strikes. Reaction time is extremely important in all defensive drills.

a

b

c

1. Stand in an open or closed fighting stance; your opponent steps forward and raises the lead hand for distraction.
2. Step back 6 to 12 inches, transferring your weight to your rear foot (figure *a*).
3. Lean backward, keeping your lead arm tight against your body for protection (figure *b*).
4. Your opponent launches the undercut punch.
5. Execute a side kick to the midsection, intercepting the incoming punch before your opponent can finish it (figure *c*).

a

b

c

COUNTERING THE REVERSE PUNCH

We provide two solid scenarios for you to practice defending effectively against a reverse-punch blitz. In addition to these, also try a ridgehand defense (see page 125).

Backfist Defense

1. Stand in an open fighting stance (figure *a*); your opponent attacks with a reverse punch toward your midsection.

2. Lean your weight back toward your rear foot and deflect the punch away with a rear palm block (figure *b*).

3. Shift your weight forward toward your front foot and execute a lead backfist to the head (figure *c*).

a

b

c

1. Stand in an open fighting stance (figure *a*); your opponent attacks with a reverse punch toward your head.
2. Step 6 to 12 inches backward with your rear foot while leaning back to avoid being hit (figure *b*).
3. Execute a side kick to the midsection (figure *c*). Other options include a lead-leg roundhouse kick to the head (figure *d;* but not from a closed stance because your opponent's punching arm will obstruct the path) and a lead-leg hook kick, wrapped around the incoming reverse punch, which can be used in both open and closed stances (figure *e*).

The previous defensive technique may be executed just as easily from a closed stance, except for the lead-leg roundhouse to the head option; this kick will get jammed because of the conflicting body positions created by the closed fighting stance.

a

b

c

d

e

COUNTERING THE RIDGEHAND STRIKE

Try these two methods for defending against ridgehand strikes.

Side Kick or Roundhouse Kick Defense

1. Stand in a closed fighting stance (figure *a*).
2. As your opponent steps forward to execute a ridgehand strike with the forward hand, step back with your rear foot and lean back to avoid being hit (figure *b*)
3. Execute a lead-leg side kick to the midsection (figure *c*) or a roundhouse kick to the head (figure *d*).

a

b

c

d

This technique can be executed from the open fighting stance as well, except for the counter roundhouse kick to the head, which will get jammed under your opponent's arm before it makes contact with its target because of the body positions and mechanics involved. When it comes to counter-attacking, the low side kick to the belt usually has the least chance of getting jammed in most situations. When in doubt counter with a side kick, unless your opponent is right up against you. The side kick can be your greatest friend at medium and far range distances.

1. Stand in an open or closed fighting stance (figure *a*).
2. The opponent steps forward with the lead foot and attempts a ridgehand with the rear hand.
3. Intercept the technique before it is completed, and execute a cross-behind backfist to the head (figure *b*).

a

b

DEFENDING AGAINST COMBINATION ATTACKS

It is very important to learn how to defend against single attacks before attempting to learn how to defend against combination attacks. The reason for this is that they are directly related and single attacks are easier to learn to defend against in the beginning. With combination attacks you have more to worry about technically.

One of the techniques that Bill Wallace trademarked in his competition days was his incredible counter-hook kick to the head. When an opponent charged or blitzed at him with punches, Bill would take a very quick step backward with his rear foot, lean his upper back away from the attack, and wrap a lead-leg hook kick around the opponent's guards or punching arm (depending on the situation), and score to the head. He literally would let opponents walk into the technique.

1. Stand in an open fighting stance; your opponent steps forward with the front foot and executes a jab punch or backfist toward your head (figures *a* and *b*).
2. Step backward with your rear foot and lean your head out of range as your opponent launches the second punch (figure *c*).
3. Execute a lead ridgehand to the head, hooking it around your attacker's punching arm (figure *d*).

As we've stressed several times in this chapter, make sure you lean back to stay out of punching range and, as a precaution, keep your rear hand up to protect your chin. Practice this drill over and over and you will find a few different ways to angle your body to score with the ridgehand. Through experimentation, you will find new ideas that will greatly help you in developing your sparring skills.

a

b

c

d

1. Stand in an open fighting stance (figure *a*); your opponent steps forward with the front foot and executes a jab punch or backfist toward your head.

2. Step backward with your rear foot (figure *b*).

a

b

3. As your opponent launches the second punch, lean your head back out of range (figure *c*).

4. Execute a lead-leg hook kick to the head (figure *d*), hooking it around your attacker's punching arm. Or execute a lead-leg side kick to the midsection (figure *e*).

c

d

(continued)

e

You can execute this defensive technique from a closed fighting stance as well. The key is to lean back just far enough that the punch will go right over the top of you while you wrap that hook kick around the incoming punch. If your opponent keeps the guards up and you are unable to score with a kick to the head, just use a side kick to the midsection. Remember, no one can protect everything at once.

7

Jamming Opponents in Close

Jamming, or smothering an attack, can be one of the best ways to not only short-circuit an aggressive attack but also to make an opponent feel frustrated and off balance. When you jam an attack, you use your arms for two jobs simultaneously—protecting the areas your opponent is targeting on your body and smothering the incoming attack. Thus, jamming and blocking are very close to the same thing—jamming is basically blocking *while* stepping into the opponent. Jamming uses the whole body to stop an attack, whereas blocking generally uses only the limbs. Now think about this: If every time you tried to throw a kick, it got stuck against your opponent's guards before you could finish it, and your opponent just smiled at you, wouldn't you feel helpless? What can you do if you're stuck on one leg while your attacker presses forward into you? Not much—maybe wait for the referee to break you up? Or even worse, wait for the hit?

This chapter shows you how to be the one who is *doing* the jamming—and this is important because jamming is a very powerful tactic to use when dealing with faster and larger opponents. We'll start by answering one of the most common questions students ask: When is the best time to try to jam an opponent?

Usually the best time to jam is when the opponent is at a close or medium range. Close range means that you are close enough to be able to kick or punch an opponent without taking a step. Medium range is when you have to take a small step to make contact with your opponent using a kick or punch. Far range is when you have to take a fairly big step or use a combination of footwork to make contact with your opponent with a kick or punch. If you try to jam from a distance greater than your arm's or leg's length, you may walk into a kick and punch, which could be very unpleasant. So think *close quarters.*

When fighting at close range, the cue to jam is when your opponent tries to chamber a leg to kick or extend a fist to punch. When fighting at medium range, the cue to jam is when your opponent makes a committed movement toward you. That committed movement could be something like a step forward or sliding footwork technique. That's when you step forward into your challenger and simultaneously smother the attack. Move in while your opponent is busy trying to complete footwork or close the gap.

In this chapter we cover scenarios you can use to practice jam kicks and punches, tactics you can apply to your current sparring skills. Practice the drills with a partner, with both of you wearing proper safety equipment (gloves, forearm guards, and shin guards are a must for practicing jamming techniques), or you will be covered in bruises from the bone-on-bone contact. Some instructors believe that sparring gear is for wimps and that you cannot learn how to fight properly without training yourself to get used to the pain of clashing arms and legs. Nothing could be further from the truth. Sparring gear will keep your limbs healthy and protected. When you are competing or doing heavy sparring, your adrenaline is usually pumping so high that you may not even feel the damage to your legs or arms until hours after or even the morning after the event. Practicing to be a tough guy is for people with ego problems or those who don't know any better. Most competitions allow protective gear anyway, so you might as well get used to wearing it while you spar and practice drills. Take the momentary pain at the competition, not during your everyday training sessions. This advice alone will greatly extend the quality of your workouts and the longevity of your martial arts competition.

As you work on the following scenarios, keep these general pointers in mind for effective jamming:

- Learn to hide behind your guards and forward shoulder by using them as shields when you step in to jam.

- Use the techniques listed here against shots directed at specific target areas:

Jamming against a rib cage shot. Use your elbows to protect your rib cage as you move in to jam. Anytime you raise your guards too high you expose your rib cage. Keep your lead arm low and tight against your body (figure 7.1).

Jamming against a head shot. When you are jamming a technique that is targeted toward your head on your blind side, raise your guards up like a boxer and tuck

Figure 7.1 Use your forearms and elbows to protect your midsection.

your chin into your shoulder (as if you fused it to your shoulder) just in case something gets through. This technique (figure 7.2a) greatly reduces any chance of your being knocked out because the power of the opponent's technique will be absorbed and dispersed throughout your upper body instead of just your head. The same technique works well for jamming a technique targeted toward the open side of your head (figure 7.2b). By tensing your muscles correctly you form your head, neck, shoulders, arms, and chest into one stable unit. Individually these elements are weak, but when used together they are strong.

a   *b*

Figure 7.2   Use your shoulders and a body lean to protect your head.

Jamming against a midriff shot. When jamming a technique that is targeted toward your belly, place both forearms against your body, keeping your lead forearm low and your rear forearm high. Make sure your arms are touching each other so that your solar plexus is adequately protected (figure 7.3).

Figure 7.3   The best way to protect the solar plexus is to put both arms, one high and one low, against your stomach.

Jamming against a straight-line shot. When jamming a technique whose trajectory is a perfect straight line, such as a jab punch or kick toward your head, keep your lead arm low and tight against your body, and lean your upper body backward while tucking your chin into your shoulder. For extra protection, keep your rear hand close to the open side of your face (figure 7.4).

Figure 7.4   A seamless body lean will put you out of reach of an incoming high kick.

- Never close your eyes while you are stepping in to jam. Some people close their eyes momentarily as they make contact with an opponent. This is a natural protective reflex that you need to retrain. You must hide behind your guards as if you're playing peek-a-boo while keeping your eyes open to avoid missing the split-second opportunity to score when your opponent is open. Also, if you close your eyes your opponent may take advantage and score. How can you defend against an opponent you can't see? There's nothing wrong with squinting your eyes a little for extra protection, but don't completely close them (unless, of course, you know how to use the force).

Flexibility for Jamming

Advanced leg flexibility is a part of Bill Wallace's system of fighting, and it played an important role in all his success in the ring. When dealing with jammers, he was able to keep his knee extremely high in chamber position, which prevented his opponents from smothering his kicks. Flexibility is also incredibly useful when facing a blitzing puncher.

Now let's get to specific scenarios to help you practice jamming methods.

1. Stand in an open fighting stance.
2. Your opponent steps forward with the front foot; likewise, you step forward with your front foot, keeping your body perfectly sideways, your lead arm down to protect your groin, and your rear arm up to protect your midsection and chin (figure *a*).
3. While your opponent is on one leg attempting to complete a roundhouse kick, execute a body-check (figure *b*).
4. Immediately follow with a lead ridgehand to the head (figure *c*). Always try to execute your ridgehand before your attacker's kicking leg hits the floor; at that point your opponent is off balance and vulnerable.

Keep your chin tucked into your shoulder in case your opponent changes his mind and decides to punch you in the head.

a

b

c

1. Stand in an open fighting stance.
2. Your opponent steps forward with a lead backfist chambered and ready to be aimed at your head (figure *a*).
3. With your front foot, step off the line of fire into a forward stance while simultaneously blocking and jamming with your rear arm (figure *b*).
4. Execute a lead undercut to the rib cage (figure *c*).

Remember that jamming and blocking are very close to the same thing. Blocking is usually just deflection of an attack, whereas jamming includes this deflection but also uses the whole body to stop the attack. You can step into your opponent from an angle or in a straight line, depending on the situation.

a

b

c

1. Stand in a closed fighting stance with your feet no wider than shoulder-width apart (figure *a*).
2. Your opponent slides the rear foot to the front foot (figure *b*).
3. As your opponent raises a knee to chamber position to execute a lead-leg roundhouse kick, you simultaneously push off of your rear foot and raise your forward knee, jamming your attacker's leg at the shin with your shin (figure *c*).
4. Execute a backfist to the head (figure *d*).

a

b

c

d

When you attempt this technique, your feet should be no wider than shoulder-width apart because you need to be able to quickly push off of your rear foot to intercept your opponent's forward leg with your forward leg. If your feet are too far apart you will have to lean all the way back on your rear foot and then propel yourself forward, which would take way too long. Keeping your feet shoulder-width apart will allow you to project your full body weight forward without having to lean back first.

1. Stand in a closed fighting stance (figure *a*).
2. Your opponent steps forward with a lead backfist chambered and ready to be aimed at your head.
3. Step forward with your front foot and turn in to a forward stance, dropping your center of gravity and your head simultaneously (figure *b*). Keep your guards up like a boxer, jamming the backfist while coming up from underneath it.

a

b

c

4. Execute an undercut punch to the rib cage with your rear hand (figure *c*), followed by another undercut with your forward hand (figure *d*).
5. Finish with a lead-leg hook kick to the head (figures *e* and *f*).

d

e

f

Once again, keep your feet about shoulder-width apart so that you can push off your rear foot quickly to move in for the jam. When you step forward make sure to drop down a few inches and then come up underneath your opponent's backfist with your head well protected. You do not want to walk straight into a backfist and get knocked out.

1. Stand in an open or closed fighting stance (figure *a*).

2. Your opponent turns the upper body in an attempt to launch a spinning hook kick to your head.

3. Step forward with your front foot into a forward stance with your guards up like a boxer, jamming the incoming kick (figure *b*).

4. Execute a lead punch (figure *c*) or a lead ridgehand (figure *d*) to the head.

Again, keep your feet about shoulder-width apart so that you can push off of your rear foot quickly to move in for the jam. Also keep your chin tucked in just in case the spinning hook kick gets through your guards.

a

b

c

d

8

Honing the Body for Competition

We train athletes hard in our karate classes, mainly through the drill scenarios like those in chapters 3 through 7. These scenarios, which include sparring techniques and strategies, are the most scientific part of our training because they are most specific to the skills and conditioning needed in a real tournament. We also require that our students attend a certain number of classes per week to be allowed to fight at a tournament that weekend. Although we can't tell you the exact number of push-ups you need to do to make you an amazing puncher, we can provide some flexibility drills and strengthening exercises that will hone your conditioning in the dojo.

In this chapter, we detail the components of a complete training program for sport karate, including sparring strategies, speed training, strength, flexibility, and endurance. Making these components a part of your training will make you a solid competitor.

PLANNING YOUR TRAINING TIME

Sport karate is not just a one-season sport. It is a sport that is practiced all year round, with tournaments scheduled throughout the year. People don't talk about preseason or postseason karate workout sessions as they do with sports like hockey, baseball, football, or other sports with one competitive season. Serious martial artists rarely experience a perfect training atmosphere simply because they usually train by themselves; they can't count on having adequate, or any, sparring partners.

Still, martial artists can categorize themselves as being in one of three basic phases to decide how to focus their training for a tournament:

Phase 1, beginners: Introduce technical skill drills, basic physical conditioning, and fight strategy.

Phase 2, intermediate competitors: Master technical skill drills and fight strategy, slightly increase endurance conditioning, and incorporate educational sparring sessions that drill specific scenarios.

Phase 3, advanced competitors: Focus on sparring and intense speed and endurance conditioning until the tournament date arrives.

How often you should train is a difficult question to answer because it is gauged by so many variables in your life, ranging from your daily work schedule and other commitments to the level of competition that you face at the tournaments you choose to enter. If you plan to compete in tournaments, get in as many days of training per week as you can. Most students generally don't train enough to be successful in tournaments. Often the average colored-belt competitor trains more than the average black belt; black belts sometimes get lazy in their training once they attain their black belt. Other variables that have a direct effect on the time you spend in training are your own mental discipline and your current level of physical fitness—endurance, strength, speed, and flexibility.

In general, colored belts should aim to train for 90 minutes or more at least three times a week to be successful at a competition. This time includes warm-up, flexibility, drills and scenarios, and any other conditioning. Black belts should aim to train for 90 to 150 minutes, four to six days a week, depending on their level of competition and level of fitness. If you are competing at a local tournament where only average competitors come out, four to five days a week should be sufficient. If you are competing at a national or international competition you should be training five or six days a week, with a least one or two days to rest your body and your mind. Seven days a week can lead to mental and physical burnout and injuries caused by insufficient recuperation time. Not all workouts have to be the same length. Ideally, you should have two to three days a week of really intense training and two to three days of easier sessions to break the work up so that you can avoid burnout. Alternate hard training days with easier days so that your body can rest and rebuild after hard training sessions.

FINDING YOUR OPTIMAL TRAINING MIX

Developing your optimal training plan is probably one of the most difficult parts of preparing for competitions. One of the most common questions competitors ask is how much of each type of training they should do: How many kicks and punches should I throw a day? Which drills should I work on the most? How many push-ups and sit-ups should I do? How many times a week should I run, and for how long at each session? These are questions that do not have one specific answer. Every fighter has different strengths and weaknesses that require an individualized approach to finding the right balance of training.

Another problem some fighters run into is how to combine technical work, speed training, and endurance training so that they do not interfere with one another. We recommend that you perform speed and endurance training on separate days from your technical training. Technical training requires that your muscles be elastic and full of energy stores and that your mind be fresh and sharp. Speed and endurance training, when done on the same day as technical training, can exhaust you physically and mentally and cause your technical training to suffer. Proper form during technical training (or skill drills) ensures mastery of a technique.

Many athletes may not have time for separate workouts for technical, speed, and endurance training, so you may find the following tip very useful for combining all three concepts into your workout as seamlessly as possible. When you are training, the order in which you perform exercises has a profound effect on how your body reacts. If you wish to combine all the types of training in the same session, do them in the following order:

1. Technical training
2. Speed training
3. Endurance training

Championship Sparring: Technical Training

Perhaps the most important part of training for tournaments is drilling the technical aspects of the sport—sparring. Sparring not only trains you on the technical and tactical aspects of fighting, but it also hones your strength and endurance. You should incorporate sparring or scenario drills into your training any day that you train.

Whether you are practicing offensive or defensive drills (such as those described in chapters 3 through 7), a good guideline is to perform each drill 10 times on each side. However, if you are learning a drill that is difficult for you, you may need to practice it 20 to 30 times on each side to get it right. Once you have some level of mastery over the drill, 10 times per side is usually sufficient. Some drills may have two to five variations depending on the situation and the stance you start in (open or closed), so you may want to do three to five repetitions of each variation to achieve even greater mastery of the drill. Remember that ultimately you have to decide what is best for you because we are all different mentally and physically. What we offer here is just a guideline for organizing your training drills.

Another excellent way to approach your training and sparring drills is to pick a technique (a specific kick or punch) and practice every variation of it (offensively and defensively) for one hour straight. In other words, you practice every possible way you can set up to score with a given technique, mixing in various footwork, fakes, feints, body positioning, jamming, and combination attacks. This is an excellent way to improve on your favorite or best technique or to improve on a technique in which you are weak. This one hour of intensity, just pounding in that single technique, will help you to develop increased reflexes beyond what regular training can give you. But don't do this intensity drill every day; do it maybe once or twice a week, or you may become really sore from repeating the same movement. You may want to try having different days for doing this drill with different techniques. For example, you could work the backfist on Tuesday and then the side kick on Friday.

Keep in mind that if you are a student in a school, you may have to do the drills in this book outside of your regular classes because your instructor may have other things for you to do. Another problem situation is that many instructors don't know how to teach sparring drills because they were never shown how to do them and don't realize their importance. A lot of schools just practice the kicks, punches, blocks, and kata, and then put on the sparring gear occasionally and try to call it traditional karate or taekwondo. Fighters know how to kick, punch, and block, but they may have no idea how to properly attack or defend. They illustrate what Bill likes to call the "throw and hope syndrome." In other words, the bout is a street fight with no strategy, just brawling at a different level. Students see a target and try to hit it on instinct alone. The proper strategic training for martial arts has been destroyed by a lot of so-called traditionalists who practice kata before anything else, claiming it is the key to the universe, but have no idea what most of the moves are for and can't explain how to get them to work in a street or sparring situation. So you ask yourself, "What's the point?"

In the ancient Orient, martial arts were developed specifically to address how to properly attack and defend. The practitioners used and practiced offensive and defensive strategies in training and in war. Their lives depended on their ability to be strategically better than their opponent. Kata was used when a warrior did not have a training partner to work with. Artists could do this exercise when they were alone to review all their techniques and keep them sharp, as boxers do when kicking and punching the heavy bag or when shadow boxing. In modern times martial artists are not trained to kill because it is not necessary, unless they are soldiers. Perhaps this is why kata has become questionable with regard to real combat and sparring. People at one point stopped taking kata so seriously, so it got watered down so badly that the whole point of it was forgotten. They started making their own patterns that are just a lot of moves in a certain order, with no particular meaning beyond being a collection of kicks, punches, and blocks.

When kata was first created it was a lethal training aid. It trained the warrior against deadly attacks, and the order of the techniques had a specific strategic meaning. Nowadays, people make their own patterns for tournaments and place moves in certain places because it looks cool to do it that way.

If you belong to a school that reflects such attitudes, don't panic. You can still benefit from your training there; you'll just have to research more things on your own: attend seminars, read books, watch videos, and find partners with proper martial arts experience to work with outside your club. When used properly, knowledge is power.

Blinding Speed and Deadly Accuracy

Developing arm and foot speed is essential for being an effective point tournament competitor. What a lot of beginning martial artists don't understand about speed is that *timing* is much more important than *brute physical speed*. But timing and speed are, without a doubt, directly related. One cannot exist without the other; if you don't grasp the relationship, your technique will fail. It is not how fast you launch your counterattack; it is more important *when* you launch it. This concept can be applied to both offensive and defensive fighting. What that means is that you can actually throw a technique too slowly or even too fast. How can a technique be too fast, you ask?

Figure 8.1, *a* through *d*, illustrates the important relationship between timing and speed. You have two fighters. The attacker plans on launching a backfist to the defender's head, and the defender plans on countering with a defensive side kick to the rib cage. Now here is what can go wrong without the correct timing. The attacker takes a small, quick step forward to get closer to the defender (figure 8.1*a*), and the defender panics and launches a kick (figure 8.1*b*), but it falls short, just barely grazing the attacker's forward guard (figure 8.1*c*). The defender's leg drops, and the attacker steps in and scores with a backfist (figure 8.1*d*).

a

b

Figure 8.1 A mistimed counterattack can get you in trouble.

c

d

Figure 8.1 *(continued)* The right move at the wrong time can set you up for a strike by your opponent.

The side kick was a correct choice to counter the attacker's backfist. So why did this happen? The answer is simple. The defender did not allow the attacker to make a full commitment to the backfist attack. By launching the side kick too early, the defender did not give the attacker the time to expose the rib cage. The defender wound up just kicking the attacker's arm instead of the rib cage. If the defender had timed the counterattack to begin when

159

the opponent committed to a deeper attack, the defender would have scored. No matter how fast you are, things can backfire on you dramatically without proper timing. In this case, the attacker's little step forward was mistaken for the real attack. Some opponents, like the one shown in figure 8.1a, will simultaneously stamp a foot as they take a step forward to fake and disturb their opponent's concentration.

To get your counterattack to work properly, you must learn how to read your opponent's body to distinguish between stalking and an actual commitment to attack. In the previous scenario the defender should have waited until the attacker's body was leaning forward with the backfist chambered (figure 8.2). Usually when an opponent leans forward into a punch and takes a deep step forward, it indicates a real commitment to attack (leaving that opponent vulnerable to a counterattack). So the deep forward step, the forward body, and the chambered backfist are the small details that you must memorize as one picture. After you have memorized how an opponent who is truly committed to an attack looks on approach, you will develop the ability to determine whether a fighter is really coming after you or just faking an attack to get a reaction.

Figure 8.2 A properly timed counterattack scores easily.

The best way to develop speed for sparring is to break quickness training into two categories: offensive speed training and defensive speed training. Drills for each type of training are presented in the next section. Keep in mind that you do not have to practice all of the drills to develop your speed. In the beginning, pick ones that you are interested in, and experiment from there.

To alleviate boredom, come back and try some that you haven't attempted yet and see what they do for you. Obviously, some practitioners will develop faster than others, and certain drills will seem more beneficial to fighters with particular fighting styles and body types. Feel free to choose drills that suit your current abilities and style. There is always room to build later on.

Before you try these drills, here are a few tips that will help you develop your speed:

- Mind and muscle relaxation is a requirement for mastery in speed training. Clear your mind of all unnecessary thoughts. Your only concern should be covering the distance to your target as fast as possible while staying loose.

- If you have access to a mirror, try doing your drill in front of the mirror so that you can visually tell whether you are relaxed.

- Keep your shoulders and neck loose and your knees slightly bent like coiled springs.

- Lightly bouncing before executing a technique or combination attack will help you to develop a relaxed state of mind, which will allow your body to follow through on the skill.

- The only time your body should tense up is on impact with the target. Think *loose, tense, loose*:
  1. Start in your fighting stance with your shoulders and hips as loose as possible.
  2. Launch your attack (while staying loose).
  3. On impact, tense your body for a split second; then relax immediately as soon as your kick or punch returns to its original position.

When Muhammad Ali was fighting back in his day, his extreme hand speed for a heavyweight was well documented and praised. The secret to this speed was the fact that he kept his whole body loose until he made contact with his punch; then he immediately became relaxed again. He also used bouncing, which he combined with incredibly deceptive footwork. This seemed to have a doubly beneficial effect for his fighting style. It kept him loose, and it was effective for defensive and offensive strategy. At one time in martial arts, taking a hard, stiff stance was favored. As athletic science progressed, the world discovered that relaxed muscles perform much more efficiently. And that's not just for martial arts or boxing; that's for all types of sports and physical activities.

Offensive Speed Training

To safely develop speed on the offensive, you should try practicing your attack combinations and footwork at three different speeds—slow, medium, and fast. Use the slow and medium speeds to warm up and coordinate your mind and body to prevent injury before sparring. Your fast speed is simply as fast as you can go. For instance, practicing a blitzing combination attack five times at slow to medium speed and then five times as fast as you can go is an excellent way to enhance your speed and avoid injury. When you do the first five more slowly, it coordinates the mind with the body and allows all the nerve paths and channels to open up, relaxing any stiff muscles and joints before you go full throttle. Even if you've done a proper warm-up and stretch before your session, if you begin with fast movements it is still possible to injure yourself. That is why you should do at least five reps at slow to regular speed to prepare the body. Otherwise it may feel as if you are grinding metal—sort of like putting on the gas and brakes at the same time.

The following drills are excellent ways to hone your offensive speed and timing. Incorporate them into your training one to two times a week.

Punching Speed Drills (Single and Combination Attacks)

Before each punch, step forward while pushing off your rear foot.

1. Execute a backfist at head level.
2. Execute a reverse punch at head or midsection level.
3. Execute a backfist at head level and execute an undercut punch at rib cage or midsection level.
4. Execute a backfist at head level and a lead-ridgehand strike at head level.
5. Execute a backfist at head level, an undercut punch at rib cage or midsection level, and a lead ridgehand strike at head level.

Kicking Speed Drills (Single and Combination Attacks)

Before each kick, step with your forward foot and slide your rear foot to your front foot.

1. Execute a lead-leg roundhouse kick at belt level or head level.
2. Execute a lead-leg side kick at belt level.
3. Execute a lead-leg hook kick at head level.
4. Execute a lead-leg roundhouse at belt level. Slide your rear foot to your front foot, and execute another lead-leg roundhouse at belt or head level or a lead-leg hook kick at head level.
5. Execute a lead-leg side kick at belt level. Slide your rear foot to your front foot and execute another lead-leg side kick at belt level, a lead-leg hook kick at head level, or a lead-leg roundhouse at belt or head level.
6. Execute a lead-leg hook kick at head level. Slide your rear foot to your front foot and execute a lead-leg side kick at belt level or a lead-leg roundhouse at belt level or head level.

Punching and Kicking Speed Drills (Combination Attacks)

Start each of these by stepping forward while pushing off your rear foot.

1. Execute a backfist at head level. Slide your rear foot to your front foot and execute a lead-leg roundhouse kick at belt or head level.

2. Execute a backfist at head level. Slide your rear foot to your front foot and execute a lead-leg side kick at belt level.

3. Execute a backfist at head level. Slide your rear foot to your front foot and execute a lead-leg hook kick at head level.

4. Execute a backfist at head level followed by a turn-back kick at the opponent's midsection or rib cage area.

5. Slide your rear foot to your front foot, and execute a lead-leg round-house kick at belt or head level. Step down and execute a backfist at head level.

6. Slide your rear foot to your front foot, and execute a lead-leg hook kick at head level. Step down and execute a backfist at head level.

7. Slide your rear foot to your front foot, and execute a lead-leg hook kick at head level. Step down and execute a lead-ridgehand strike at head level.

Shadowboxing or kicking is another excellent way of developing speed and endurance simultaneously. Practice 4 to 10 one- to three-minute rounds per workout, depending on your current physical condition.

Defensive Speed Training

To develop speed on the defensive, have a training partner throw attacks at your target areas, especially in the beginning. Once you get started and understand the drills and the timing involved, all you need is a good imagination. When working with a partner, you should pad yourself up with protective gear to prevent accidental injury.

Punching Speed Drills

1. Step back with your rear foot while leaning your head out of range, and execute a counter-lead ridgehand strike at head level.

2. Execute a lead high block and then execute a rear undercut punch at rib cage or midsection level.

3. With your feet no more than shoulder-width apart, pretend your opponent is going to slide up to throw a kick. In your mind picture the move forward. As soon as you see that move, push hard off your rear foot and execute a backfist at head level.

Kicking Speed Drills

1. Step back with your rear foot, lean your upper body backward out of range, and execute a side kick at rib cage or midsection level.

2. Step back with your rear foot, lean your upper body backward out of range, and execute a lead-leg roundhouse kick at head level.

3. Step back with your rear foot, lean your upper body backward out of range, and execute a lead-leg hook kick at head level.

4. Starting with your feet no more than shoulder-width apart, execute a turn-back kick at rib cage or midsection level.

Brute Physical Speed

Combining martial arts with cross-training has become extremely popular because of its effectiveness in conditioning competitors for fighting matches. Unfortunately, practicing just the movements of karate cannot completely develop an athlete to full potential. There are some exercises that are better designed for achieving certain goals. For example, you cannot develop maximum strength and stability in your arms through punching alone. That is why many martial arts schools have their students do knuckle push-ups. Many fighters also like to use barbells and weights (that is, resistance training) to increase the power and speed in their arms. Resistance training will help develop an explosive snap in your punch. Lifting heavy weights with low repetitions (1 to 10 reps) develops explosive power, whereas lifting light weights with high repetitions (15 to 30 reps) builds muscle endurance. Both are very important for the sport karate competitor.

Some martial artists also claim that weight training for the legs is quite beneficial; others disagree, claiming that it makes their kicks slower and less snappy. The legs, however, are a little different than the arms. The legs are already strong because they support the whole body's weight every day. When you throw a kick one leg has to support everything, so you could say the legs get quite a good workout already compared to the arms. Now the catch is that speed and strength are worth nothing if you do not have good endurance. This is what endurance training (see pages 168 to 172) is for.

Endurance Strength for Kicking

1. Facing a partner, clasp each other's opposite hand and then place your free hand on top to reinforce your grip (figure 8.3a).

2. Raise your knee to chamber position (make sure the toes on your supporting leg are facing the opposite direction of the kick to prevent injury and to insure proper form) (figure 8.3b).

3. Execute 10 to 50 roundhouse kicks as high as you can go without dropping your foot to the floor.

Always return your kick back to the chamber position with a quick, whip-like snap. Keep your knee as high as possible while maintaining good balance and stability. Look at your foot while executing the kicks to help develop proper form.

Perform the same drill, but replace the roundhouse kick with a side kick or hook kick. You may also want to vary your sets, mixing all three of those kicks together while simultaneously varying the height of each kick to hit low, middle, and high target areas. Instead of performing this drill in sets, you can use a stop-

a   *b*

Figure 8.3 These partner drills for strength and endurance can also be done using the back of a chair.

watch and do the exercise in 1- to 3-minute rounds depending on your current physical condition. Always work your way up slowly to prevent injury.

Strength for Kicking

1. Facing a partner, clasp each other's opposite hands and then place your free hand on top to reinforce your grip.
2. Raise your knee to chamber position (make sure the toes on your supporting leg are facing the opposite direction of the kick to prevent injury and to ensure proper form.
3. Hold out a roundhouse kick or a side kick as high as you can for an interval of 30 seconds to 2 minutes depending on your current physical condition. Always start with a short amount of time and then work your way up so your body can become accustomed to the exercise.

You can vary this exercise by holding your kick out at different heights to work different muscle groups.

Optimal Flexibility

Another physical attribute that has a great effect on your speed is flexibility. If your muscles are rigid, they will not perform as optimally as flexible muscle tissue will. If your muscles are elastic and flexible, your kicks and punches will have more snap to them. When you have snap, you have speed.

Some athletes think that if they develop extreme flexibility, they will lack power because they will be too "rubbery," that there will be nothing stable behind their technique. The reality of it is that if you combine flexibility training with strength and endurance training, you will have no problems developing the speed and power that you need. Muscles can be powerful and extremely flexible at the same time.

We recommend performing flexibility training, in other words, stretching, before doing any speed training. Kicking and punching at great speeds before doing a proper warm-up can lead to severe injury, which any sane person wishes to avoid. Stretching can keep you from tearing muscles, ligaments, and tendons that are needed for everyday living, never mind extreme martial arts practice and competition. Always train smart. Remember that the body does only what it can do in its current physical state. Don't expect your body to do something that it isn't physically prepared for. Warm up before practicing techniques.

Hamstring and Groin Stretch

1. Sitting on the floor, with your legs spread apart about 90 degrees or more, pull your head down toward your right foot. Hold for 20 to 30 seconds.
2. Repeat the same on your left side.
3. Finally grab your ankles and pull your head down toward the floor. Hold for 20 to 30 seconds.

Adductor and Groin Stretch

1. From a seated position, start with your legs approximately 90-degrees apart and your hands behind your back for support.
2. Pretend one ankle is pinned to the floor and push forward with the opposite leg until your legs spread apart further. Hold this position for 20 to 30 seconds.
3. Repeat the above procedure until your legs are spread as far as you can go.

Upper Body Stretches

The upper body, unlike the lower body, needs a less dramatic stretching routine to warm up to a fully functional range of motion in the joints.

1. Perform 5 to 10 (in each direction, for each limb) of the following: arm circles, neck circles, and torso rotations. Five rotations in each direction is sufficient unless you are very stiff. Always practice rotations slowly and smoothly and avoid jerky motions. This will protect the joints and surrounding muscle tissue from injury.

2. Perform 5 to 10 torso bends to the front, rear, and sides. Only bend until you feel a healthy stretch in the muscles. Rotations and bends should feel good; there should never be any real pain.

Developing Reflexive Speed

Reflexive speed is how fast your brain responds to external stimuli and communicates this to your weapons—your hands and feet. During sparring or combat, the mind responds to visual stimuli. Once these data are transmitted to the brain, the brain has to analyze the data and decide what its response will be. Once the brain has made a decision on how to proceed, signals are sent to the necessary muscle groups required to control your body. The process sounds simple, but it is one of the most important parts of fighting. If you have poor or slow reflexes, you will not perform well, end of story. Fortunately, there are many drills and exercises you can use to improve reflex speed. They are, without a doubt, all similar to one another. The key is to choose a few that you feel comfortable with and enjoy doing.

Counterattack drills are probably the most realistic and efficient way to develop reflexive speed because they are the closest to actual fighting situations. Study and practice the drills and exercises in chapters 5, 6, and 7. They will greatly develop and enhance your reflexive speed.

Random target drills are another excellent way to develop your reflexes. Have a partner lower and raise a target in different positions while you react. Hit the target only when it comes to a full stop. Let your partner change the position and then react and strike again. Your partner can use one or two targets. Once you gain proficiency, make your partner go faster and see if you can keep up. Try one- to three-minute rounds. To make it more challenging and more interesting, have your partner move around the room as you continue attacking the target, or have your partner charge at you while you back up and counterattack the target.

Dodgeball is not only fun, but it also develops reflex speed. In this game, you are forced to concentrate on an object that is about to make contact with you, and you must make split-second decisions on how to avoid the attack. Although playing dodgeball is not as complex as doing counterattack drills with a partner, it is a great way to introduce a beginner to this concept.

Tag is another great game to use especially when training children. Tag requires split-second decision making, which in turn develops reflex speed. The concept of a hand reaching out and trying to touch you is similar to that of someone trying to punch you. This drill can also be used as an easy and nonintimidating introduction to sparring.

Cardiorespiratory Conditioning

In all organized sporting events there are variables that determine what type of physical conditioning an athlete needs for success at a given level. In most point karate tournaments 90 to 120 seconds is the average length of a match. Unfortunately, there is no way of knowing in advance how many matches you will compete in or the amount of time you will have between matches at a given tournament. Physical conditioning is important because one must always be prepared for the unknown.

In the fight game, endurance is king. As soon as you start getting tired, your speed and strength start to dwindle. You need to develop your heart muscle and lungs because they supply all your other muscles with fresh, oxygenated blood. When you have poor endurance, the oxygenation process is greatly hampered.

Endurance conditioning for point fighting is nowhere as extreme as it is for full-contact fighting. Although endurance training is important, speed and timing in executing techniques are the main ingredients for success in sport karate. The fight is over as soon as someone scores enough points (usually three or four) to win the match or the time is up for the round. Each bout lasts one round, which is usually 90 to 120 seconds long; every time a point is scored the center judge stops the match to award the point, giving the fighters time to recuperate. Another variable that allows sport karate participants to do less endurance training than full-contact participants is that sport karate allows only very light contact to the target areas. In full-contact martial arts, to continually receive and dish out full-power shots, you must have high physical endurance or you risk being seriously hurt or even knocked out. Full-contact martial arts competitions are similar to boxing matches in that the fighters are allowed to hit as hard as they want to designated target areas, one fight may last many rounds depending on the type of competition, and the fight is not stopped during the round unless the fighters break the rules.

So a sport karate competition allows a competitor to compete in an environment that is less stressful and more controlled that of full-contact competitions. If you are a new martial arts competitor, we highly recommend that you try competing in sport karate tournaments before attempting to fight in a full-contact event; if you are not accustomed to competing, starting at the far end of the scale might be too intense. A point competition is an excellent way to warm up to the idea of competing full-contact. At least this way you'll know beforehand whether you mind getting hit by a perfect stranger who does not care about your personal well-being.

Fighting in the club and fighting in a tournament are two different things entirely. You have to watch out for number one—yourself. And always, and we mean *always*, follow the rules of the tournament that you are competing in. The rules are there for your safety and your opponent's safety. Playing fair is how you show respect to your opponents and the way you gain respect from your opponents and judges. Nobody respects a dirty fighter except in a street fight, and in that case there are no rules to respect.

Most of the literature on endurance training for martial arts is for full-contact fighting, not for point fighting. Although speed and timing are paramount in point competitions, a serious competitor should not overlook intense endurance training. Even during a match that lasts one round you can become extremely tired when facing a well-trained opponent. Whenever you become fatigued you are more apt to make stupid mistakes or mistime attacks and counterattacks.

Some martial arts instructors think that it is the students' responsibility to perform conditioning exercises on their own time, and that includes stretching and warm-up exercises. Unfortunate as this may be, it is a reality that a lot of competitors have to face. The average martial arts school does not give athletes everything they need to become a champion. To excel, you must take charge of and be responsible for your own training. Attending class on a regular basis and training at home, at a local gym, in a park, or even in your own backyard are all things that you have to consider doing to enhance your competitive edge.

Many students say that they don't have the time to do extra training. In most cases this is far from the truth. For example, the average person spends a good deal of free time in front of the television set at home. If you are interested in improving endurance without interfering with your television time, we recommend that you purchase a stationary bike for the TV room. Ride for 30 minutes per session two to five times a week, depending on the level of endurance you wish to acquire. Find a bike that runs smoothly and quietly (bikes with magnetic tension control tend to be quiet) so that you do not bother others in your home or building. Regardless of what you do, in the end, you must make some sort of extra commitment if you wish to excel.

Two types of endurance training will benefit the point fighter: aerobic and anaerobic.

Aerobic Fitness for Endurance and Recovery

In the fight game, aerobic fitness enables you to recover quickly between heavy exchanges and prepare for the next clashing of arms and legs. If you're a beginner, it is more important to concentrate on aerobic fitness than anaerobic fitness. To improve anaerobic fitness, it has been proven that you must first improve aerobic fitness.

The most popular exercises that fighters use for developing aerobic endurance are running, skipping rope, bicycling, and doing jumping jacks. For best results, start by performing one or more of these exercises for 20 to 30 continuous minutes, three times a week. After several weeks, work your way up to five sessions a week. Listen to your body. If you are feeling too tired during your karate workouts, cut down the number of endurance sessions per week.

Running.   Running is probably the most traditional and most popular cardiovascular exercise among fighters and competitors. Always wear proper running shoes that feel very comfortable. If you get blisters on your feet from your running shoes, it means they are inappropriate for running. Do not use cross-training shoes for running. If you are serious about running, you may have to invest $90 (US) or more to get a pair of shoes that provide the support needed to prevent injuries. You may want to go to a specialty running store to get fitted for your shoes; such specialty shops often train their employees on how to fit shoes to suit the way you run, your body build, your foot's shape, and so forth. Cheap or ill-fitting running shoes can cause foot, ankle, knee, back, or hip problems as well as shin splints. The shoe must be designed to provide proper support for the arch of the foot as well as maximum shock absorption. Remember that every time you take a stride forward, up to six times your full body weight is transferred to one foot. During a 20- to 30-minute running session you may put this stress on each foot hundreds or thousands of times.

Athletes who are very heavy need to be careful when engaging in running exercises because their greater weight means that more stress is applied to the body every time each foot makes impact with the ground. Some people believe only obese people have these stress problems because of their lack of muscle tone; however, very muscular athletes, such as bodybuilders over 200 pounds, can suffer the same problems if their skeletal structure is not properly supported.

A good sign that your running shoes are worthy of running in is that they make you feel as if you are running on pillows. If you take your first run in your new shoes, and your feet and legs get tired and sore before you are out of breath, that is telltale sign that the shoes are bad news. The best shoes still will leave you out of breath but without body pain during your run. Another good tip is to run only on flat and even surfaces to avoid undue stress on your ankles and knees.

Some athletes with pronated feet (meaning the feet turn inward and downward when walking or running) or flat feet (meaning they have no arch in their foot) need to visit a good podiatrist (foot doctor) and get arch supports made for their shoes. Just a warning: Good orthotics can cost hundreds of dollars but are sometimes necessary for proper arch support.

Skipping Rope.   Skipping rope is one of the most effective ways of developing your cardiovascular endurance. It also develops upper- and lower-body coordination, arm endurance, and of course, strength and stability in the legs. Always wear proper running shoes that are designed for the constant impact of jumping up and down. The better cushioned and supported your feet are, the less chance you have of developing injury.

Bicycling.   Bicycling is a great way to improve your cardiovascular endurance. Like the other aerobic exercises, it contributes to the overall leg strength and stability required for kicks and powerful footwork. The advantage of using a bicycle or stationary bike over other traditional endurance exercises is that the exercise is low impact. Injured athletes with multiple joint problems can still improve their cardiovascular system without incurring the same amount of stress experienced when running or skipping rope. With a stationary bike, you can choose the exact intensity of your ride simply by adjusting the tension knob. For example, if you have bad knees you would use a low tension to prevent further injury. When the tension is too high an injured joint will feel as though it's grinding metal and become inflamed. Exercise increases blood flow to injured areas of the body and promotes faster healing; but if the injured area is overstrained, swelling, inflammation, and further injury may follow.

When adjusting the intensity, select a point where you feel comfortable and free of pain in the injured area. Know the difference between feeling pain and feeling healthy physical exertion. Many beginners have a difficult time differentiating between the two. Unfortunately, you can only learn this through trial and error. To increase your cardiovascular endurance, you'll need to lengthen your bike sessions to 30 to 45 minutes, three to five times a week. If you find your legs are too sore in the beginning and that the soreness is affecting your karate workouts, either reduce the time of the bike sessions or do fewer bike sessions a week.

Jumping Jacks. Jumping jacks are a popular form of exercise in the military and in martial arts schools, and they are used as a means of improving cardiovascular endurance. They're popular because they can be done in a small, closed space with minimal equipment and setup. Running, on the other hand, requires much larger spaces. Jumping jacks work both the arms and the legs, providing maximum circulation throughout the body. You can also do multiple variations of the exercise to alleviate possible stress caused by repetitive motion. You can combine running on the spot with jumping jacks as well. Most karate practitioners train barefoot, so any more than 5 minutes of jumping jacks done barefoot can be counterproductive. If you are barefoot, use jumping jacks only as a brief warm-up exercise and not for extreme endurance training. Shin splints are a common result of long jumping jack sessions in bare feet; therefore, use a padded floor and good running shoes when doing long sessions of jumping jacks.

Anaerobic Fitness and Speed Endurance

Anaerobic fitness is essential in the fight game. Anaerobic means "without oxygen." Thus, the anaerobic part of your fight occurs during heavy exchanges with your opponent when you don't have time to breathe between every movement. The technical term is *performance in oxygen deficit*. Basically your body is working anaerobically when you are kicking and punching without taking a breath inward. Just think how difficult it would be to inhale and exhale for every movement you make in a heavy exchange with your opponent. It is basically impossible, so this is why you need the ability to perform while in oxygen deficit. Sprinting and combination attack training are the main exercises used to develop anaerobic fitness among fighters.

Sprinting. Because of the intensity of sprinting, rather than 20 to 30 minutes, a competitor should only do 5 to 10 minutes of sprinting drills in a session no more than three times a week. Considering that karate requires a lot of kicking, you do not want to burn out your legs for all the other drills that are necessary in training. Make sure that you are properly warmed up before attempting sprinting drills, because they are very strenuous and involve powerful movements of the large muscle groups in the legs. It is very easy to damage these muscles when sprinting. The strain that a quick take-off can put on your legs in going from a stationary position to maximum speed can be a disaster. If you are new to sprinting, gradually work up your speed in sprinting bouts; your legs may not be able to handle the initial stress of a quick take-off. There is no point in injuring yourself for nothing. Better safe than sorry.

Combination Attacks. It is a scientific fact that there is no better way to develop a skill than to actually practice the skill. Anaerobic development for the martial artist will come mainly from the actual practice of combination attacks or drills at a medium to high intensity level. Practicing combination techniques (that is, a combination of three or more techniques) in rapid succession will increase your anaerobic capacity. (Refer to chapter 6 for drills on combination attacks.)

9

Stifling Opponents' Attacks and Creating Scoring Opportunities

Creating openings and scoring opportunities on your opponent is the purpose of having and executing a strategy. When you create openings, whether in a defensive posture or an attack posture, you must be able to instantaneously see and attack that opening. In this chapter we'll show you how to create openings on your opponents and then use these openings to score.

CREATING OPENINGS

As you have learned from chapters 3 through 7, there are many ways of creating and recognizing scoring opportunities. First, check out your opponent's stance to see what openings are already there. Then, by looking at the stance, you can determine what new openings you can create. Ask the following questions as you observe your opponent:

- Where are the hands and how does your opponent move them to guard and strike?

- Does your opponent stand with the left or right side forward? Openings vary depending on which side the fighter faces and which stance the fighter uses. The hand and arm positions, as well as the targets, also vary according to stance.

- Is the weight forward or back? If the weight is forward, then it could mean that your opponent is an offensive fighter. If the weight is on the rear foot, it could mean your opponent is a defensive fighter.

- Does your opponent shift from side to side? This is an important indicator of timing. You want to see how you can upset that timing.

- Is your opponent a defensive or offensive fighter? Some fighters wear down the competition by applying and maintaining the pressure. Their opponents grow weary and go on the defensive. The trouble with this type of strategy is that the person who is applying the pressure may take a lot of punishment along the way. Remember, there are no points for defense. It is better to hit than to be hit. Be prepared for the pressure fighters; they are brutes. When you are fighting hard contact, don't be in a big hurry. Take your time to set up and execute your techniques—you'll need your endurance. Practice relaxed, controlled movements. If you get tired, you get slow, weak, and more susceptible to a knockout. When you're fighting in rounds, rhythm is very important because of the combinations being used.

- How does your opponent defend? Throw a quick and simple technique and notice exactly how the fighter defends, moves, and blocks. Does he back up to defend? Does she use the front hand, rear hand, or both to block? How does he move the head? Does she move the head away from the weapon? Does he close his eyes?

USING OPENINGS TO SCORE

One of the most important aspects of sparring is to know what techniques to execute when you have created or found that opening in your opponent. Determining the best technique involves answering two simple questions:

- Am I a kicker or a puncher?
- What techniques are the quickest and most efficient for me to throw?

You need to get to that opening with the quickest technique available to you, so your answers to these questions will tell you which techniques to execute. If you have to stop and think, the opening will no longer be there; you don't have a lot of time to ponder what technique to use. Also remember that your opponent is trying to figure *you* out. Finally, use a simple and quick technique because *you* want to be the first to score to upset your opponent's mind-set.

To me (Bill), sparring has always been very simple. Because of the injury to my right knee, I used only five techniques in my entire career. My kicking movements included a side kick, roundhouse kick, and hook kick. My only two hand techniques were a backfist (jab) and a hook punch. I threw each of these techniques from the left side (with my left hand and foot) to protect my right knee. This worked out perfectly for me, since I am left-handed and left-legged.

Standing sideways in a horse stance was easy, safe, and comfortable for me. Also, from this position I could throw any of my techniques offensively or defensively. By using the skills I was best at, I was able to score points quickly. The same is true for any competitor. Discover what skills are your best assets and continue to hone them.

The backfist is many competitors' best skill, and it is worth improving. The backfist is probably one of the first weapons you were taught. It is also the number one point-fighting technique in the world because it is fast and easy to throw. If you watch a boxing match, you'll notice how the jab sets up all the combinations. The jab also keeps your opponent away from you. The jab in boxing is the same as a backfist in karate. Just ask Muhammad Ali.

If your backfist is effective, then you are able to throw your other weapons. Once you throw the backfist, your opponent's hands will come up to protect the face, and now you've created an opening. The first combination we all learned was the backfist (jab), and then we learned the reverse punch, right? We see this combination work time and time again because the speed of the jab makes it so difficult to defend against.

The front-leg roundhouse kick is just like a jab with your foot. It's a great kick to throw to the midsection because it is extremely quick, which makes it difficult to block. When you throw the kick to the midsection, your opponent's hands must come down to try to block the kick, which will then create openings.

When your opponent begins to guess where you will attack next, it gets even easier to create openings and set up combinations. You now have the opponent on the defensive. Again, watch what your opponent does to defend. Note how, when, and with what your opponent blocks.

Again, to be a good strategist you need to know what works for you. Pick your best techniques and work them so that they are effective for you, both offensively and defensively. It does you no good to know what to do if you are unable to do it. All techniques can work; you just need to set them up. There is always an opening somewhere when you're sparring; you must find it or, better yet, use the techniques from the beginning of this chapter to observe your opponent and create the opening.

There is always someone out there who is faster. There is always someone stronger. There are those who have better technique, more flexibility, and more intelligence; but no one ever has to be sneakier than you. I used to use the word *experience,* but then I got old. I don't like that word now because it denotes my age. Know how your opponent reacts, and you will be ahead of the game. Good luck, and remember to keep that leg up.

Adjusting to Specific Fighting Styles

When you spar in tournaments or in the dojo, you will often meet opponents who create a challenge for your specific fighting style (see chapter 2). These match-ups are what we like to call *oddball combinations.* The match-ups may involve two competitors who use the same styles (such as a counterfighter against another counterfighter), but they have dramatic differences in height or weight. In the following pages I have listed some of these oddball combinations with some tips on what you can do to remove some of the awkwardness of the situation and turn it into an actual fighting strategy. This in itself will teach you how to recognize the weaknesses in your own style or body type and turn them into an advantage against your opponent.

Shorter Versus Taller

If you are shorter than your opponent, it can be very intimidating for you. Taller fighters have more reach and generally more body weight and power behind their techniques. Scoring to the head with a kick or punch on a taller opponent is more difficult as well because you have to stretch farther to hit your target. If your opponent has wide shoulders and steps into you, it is easy to get your kick caught on the shoulders, which in turn can make you lose your balance and land you on your butt. So what can you do to even up the odds? Shorter people can sometimes move faster because they typically have less body weight to move. If this is true in your case, your main goal is to either keep out reach or stay inside close enough to jam or smother the leg or arm before your attacker can finish the technique. This strategy is similar to that of the dancer or runner style (see chapter 2). More often than not, staying stationary against a larger and stronger opponent can be suicide. Making your opponent chase you while you change escape angles and then striking as your opponent tries to follow you can keep you safe (see "Using Defensive Footwork," chapter 5). Or you may try blitzing at your opponent with fast, penetrating combinations at a moment of weakness. Jamming and then countering while your opponent is off balance can be very effective against kicks and punches as well. (See chapter 7 for some examples of jamming techniques.)

Taller Versus Shorter

If you are taller than your opponent, your main goal is to keep your adversary from getting inside of your punches and kicks. A smaller opponent is best kept at long range. A shorter fighter who is well trained will try to blitz at you to smother your techniques and get behind your knee or elbow, rendering your kicks and punches useless. Use your long reach to keep your opponent frustrated and at bay. By keeping smaller opponents just inside your kicking and punching range, you can be your own best friend; but if you let them get close enough so that you're inside of their reach, you lose the advantage because your longer limbs have a greater chance of being jammed.

Offensive Versus Offensive Competitor

When two offensive fighters square off with each other, it can look very scrappy. They sometimes have the tendency to attack at the same time and wind up jamming each other; then the referee has to pull them apart because neither one will back off to set up for some other strategy. Offensive fighters are very territorial and do not like to back up. They will fight for every forward inch that they can get. So if you are an offensive fighter squaring off against another offensive fighter, first you must understand that you may not be the superior offensive fighter in every situation. You need to train yourself not to just move forward in a straight line. You must learn lateral and circular footwork techniques to precede your attacks. This can temporarily unbalance your opponent before you attack and make the defender less likely to launch an attack or counterattack as you approach. And instead of always engaging attacks, you can use lateral and circular evasive techniques as your opponent attacks. This can slow opponents down by making them waste energy charging after someone who disappears when they attack. If you use lateral and circular evasive techniques to wear down your opponents, they will be selective about what they throw, which in turn can buy you some time with pressure fighters who kick and punch nonstop.

Counterattacking Versus Counterattacking Competitor

When two defensive fighters face off, the result is usually two fighters just standing there waiting for the other to make the first move. They don't want to budge because it is against their nature. To deal with this situation, you must learn the art of luring (see chapter 4), which involves first throwing a technique that looks desirable enough for your opponent to try to counter. When the other fighter is lured into countering your setup technique, you must be ready immediately with the appropriate counter to the incoming counterattack.

Index

Note: The italicized *f* following page
numbers refers to figures.

A

adductor stretch 166
aerobic fitness 169–171
aggressive competitors 13
anaerobic fitness 171–172
arcing shots, defending 121–122, 122*f*
arm position defenses
    against blitzes 121–122, 122*f*, 123*f*
    for jamming 143–145, 143*f*, 144*f*,
        145*f*

B

backfist
    creating openings with 175
    defending against 20–23, 123–127
    as defense
        against reverse punch 29, 131
        against ridgehand strike 42, 136
        against roundhouse kick
            combinations 114–118
        against side kick 56, 104–105
        against side kick combinations
            112–113
    described 16–18
    drawing drills 76–77
    from fake side kick 81
    jamming 147, 150–151
    offensive tactics 18–19
bicycling 170–171
blitzes
    defending against 120–122, 122*f*,
        123*f*, 136–140
    defined 38, 120
body lean defenses
    against blitzes 121–122, 122*f*, 123*f*,
        137–140
    for jamming 143–145, 144*f*, 145*f*
bouncing 161

C

cardiorespiratory conditioning 168–172
champion, defined 5
chiropractors 6–7
closed stance
    described 11, 11*f*
    drawing drills 68–69, 72–73, 76–77
combination attacks
    blitzes, countering 121–122, 122*f*,
        123*f*, 136–140
    as endurance training 167, 172
    kicks, countering
        general strategies 94, 110–111
        roundhouse combinations 110–
            111, 114–118
        side kick combinations 112–113
    speed drills 162–163
commitment, to training 2–5
competitions. *See* opponents;
        tournaments
conditioning. *See* training
control, in competitive fights 6, 31
costs, of tournaments 4
counterattacking competitors. *See*
        defensive competitors
counterattacks. *See* defensive tactics
cross-training 164

D

dancer competitors 14
defensive competitors
    described 13
    drawing 66–67
    paired in tournament 177
defensive footwork 94–97, 95*f*, 96*f*
defensive tactics
    against blitzes 121–122, 122*f*, 123*f*,
        136–140
    against combination-kick attacks
        general strategies 94, 110–111

defensive tactics *(continued)*
    roundhouse combinations 110–111, 114–118
    side kick combinations 112–113
    against single kicks
        hook kick 61–64, 106–109
        roundhouse kick 46–49, 97–103
        side kick 55–56, 104–105
    against single punches
        backfist 20–23, 123–127
        general strategies 120–122
        reverse punch 27–29, 131–133
        ridgehand strike 40–42, 134–136
        undercut punch 34, 128–130
    speed training 163–164, 167
dodgeball, for speed training 167
dragon competitors 14
drawing
    described 66–67, 92
    drills 68–79
drills
    blitz defenses 136–140
    combination-kick attack defenses 110–118
    drawing 68–79
    fake kick 81–91
    jamming 146–152
    single kick defenses
        hook kick 106–109
        roundhouse kick 97–103
        side kick 104–105
    single punch defenses
        backfist 123–127
        reverse punch 131–133
        ridgehand strike 134–136
        undercut punch 128–130

E

endurance training 164–165, 165*f*, 168–172
energy levels 7

F

fake kicks
    described 80, 92
    drills 81–91
    programming opponents for 92
faking. *See* fake kicks
fear 6
fighting styles
    of opponents 176–177
    types of 12–14
fights, real versus competitive 6, 31

flexibility
    in defending punches 121
    in jamming 145
    stretches for 165–167
footwork 94–97, 95*f*, 96*f*
front stance 10, 10*f*

G

goal setting 7–8
groin stretch 166

H

hamstring stretch 166
hand strikes. *See* punches
head shots, jamming 143–144, 144*f*
heel, striking with 51
height, of opponents 176–177
hook kick
    defending against 61–64, 106–109
    as defense
        against backfist 20
        against blitzes 138–140
        against hook kick 62, 106–107
        against reverse punch 27, 132
        against roundhouse kick 48, 102–103
        against undercut punch 34, 128–129
    described 56–57
    fake 88–92
    from fake roundhouse 84–85
    from fake side kick 82–83
    jamming 152
    offensive tactics 58–60

J

jamming
    to buy time 61
    described 142
    drills 146–152
    general strategies 143–145, 143*f*, 144*f*, 145*f*
    timing of 142
joint problems 7
jumping jacks 171
jumping rope 170

K

kata 157
kicks. *See also specific kicks*
    countering 94, 110–111
    versus punches 120
    speed drills 162–164
    strength training drills 164–165, 165*f*

L

luring. *See* drawing

M

master competitors 14
midriff shots, jamming 144, 144*f*
Muhammad Ali 161
muscle problems 7

N

nutritionists 7

O

oddball combinations 176–177
offensive competitors 177
offensive tactics
  kicks
    hook kick 58–60
    roundhouse kick 44–45
    side kick 52–55
  punches
    backfist 18–19
    reverse punch 25–26
    ridgehand strike 38–40
    undercut punch 32–34
  speed training 161–163
openings
  attacking to score 175–176
  creating 174
open stance
  described 12, 12*f*
  drawing drills 70–71, 74–75
opponents
  observing 160, 174
  oddball combinations 176–177
oxygen deficit 171

P

performance in oxygen deficit 171
physiotherapists 6–7
pressure fighters 13
protective gear 105, 142–143
punches. *See also* blitzes; *specific punches*
  countering 120–122, 122*f*, 123*f*
  versus kicks 120
  speed drills 162–163
push step (backward) 95, 95*f*

Q

quick retreat 96, 96*f*

R

random target drills 167
relaxation 161

reverse punch
  defending against 27–29, 131–133
  as defense 63, 108–109
  described 24
  offensive tactics 25–26
  versus undercut punch 30
rib cage shots, jamming 143, 143*f*
ridgehand strike
  defending against 40–42, 134–136
  as defense
    against backfist 23, 125
    against blitzes 137
    against hook kick 63, 108–109
    against reverse punch 28
    against roundhouse kick 46, 98–99
  described 36–37
  offensive tactics 38–40
roundhouse combinations, countering 110–111, 114–118
roundhouse kick
  creating openings with 175
  defending against 46–49, 97–103
  as defense
    against backfist 20, 126–127
    against reverse punch 27, 132
    against ridgehand strike 41, 134–135
  described 42–43
  drawing drills 68–73
  fake 84–87
  from fake hook kick 88–89, 92
  from fake side kick 82–83
  high, from fake low roundhouse 86–87
  jamming 146, 148–149
  offensive tactics 44–45
runner competitors 14
running 170

S

Schwarzenegger, Arnold 5
scoring 175–176
seven essential techniques. *See also specific techniques*
  backfist 16–23
  hook kick 56–64
  reverse punch 24–29
  ridgehand strike 36–42
  roundhouse kick 42–49
  side kick 50–56
  undercut punch 30–35
shadowboxing 163

side kick. *See also* stopping side kick
  defending against 55–56, 104–105
  as defense
    against backfist 20, 126–127
    against blitzes 138–140
    against reverse punch 27, 132
    against ridgehand strike 41, 134–135
    against roundhouse combinations 110–111
    against undercut punch 34, 130
  described 50–51
  drawing drills 74–75, 78–79
  fake 81–83
  from fake hook kick 90–91
  offensive tactics 52–55
side kick combinations, countering 112–113
side stance 10, 10*f*
sidestepping 97
skipping rope 170
sparring 156–157
sparring gear 105, 142–143
speed
  defensive training 163–164
  developing 160–161
  flexibility and 165–167
  offensive training 161–163
  reflexive training 167
  strength training and 164–165, 165*f*
  timing and 157–160, 158*f*, 159*f*, 160*f*
sprinting 172
stances
  described 10–12, 10*f*, 11*f*, 12*f*
  in drawing drills 67
  in fake kicks 80
stopping side kick
  against hook kick 61
  against roundhouse kick 47, 100–101
  against side kick 55

straight-line shots
  defending 121, 122*f*
  jamming 144–145, 145*f*
street fights, versus competitive 6, 31
strength training 164–165, 165*f*
stretches 166–167
strikes. *See* punches
success, commitment and 2
Superfoot System, described 12–13

T
tag, for speed training 167
technical training 156–157
time conflicts 4–5, 169
timing
  for jamming 142
  speed and 157–160, 158*f*, 159*f*, 160*f*
tournaments
  cost of 4
  opponents in 176–177
  point versus full-contact 168
  readiness to compete in 7–8
  selecting 8
training
  amount required 3, 154–155
  commitment to 2–5, 169
  comprehensive nature of 5–6
  optimal mix 155–156
  technical 156–157
trajectory techniques 16

U
undercut punch
  defending against 34, 128–130
  as defense 22, 124
  described 30–31
  offensive tactics 32–34
upper body stretches 166–167
uppercut, versus undercut punch 30

W
weight-related problems 7

About the Authors

Adam Gibson has been a martial arts competitor and instructor for the past 15 years. A student of Bill "Superfoot" Wallace for the past four years, he is the only Canadian instructor certified to teach the Superfoot System.

Gibson holds advanced black belts in both taekwondo and hapkido as well as in the Superfoot System. He has run his own martial arts studio for a decade and has made dozens of martial arts instructional videos. He is also the author of two other books, *Taekwondo Sparring Strategies: For the Ring and the Street* and *Advanced Taekwondo: Sparring and Hapkido Techniques*. Gibson lives in Ontario, Canada.

You can reach Adam via e-mail at videoman@idirect.com or visit his Web site, www.adamgibsontkd.com, for videos and seminar information.

Bill "Superfoot" Wallace is a martial arts legend. Known as "Superfoot" for his awesome left leg, he retired as the Professional Karate Association (PKA) undefeated middleweight champion after 15 years of competing in both full-contact and point tournaments. During his competitive years, Wallace captured the U.S. Championships title three times, the U.S. Karate Association (USKA) Grand Nationals title three times, and the Top Ten Nationals title twice.

Wallace was named to *Black Belt* magazine's Hall of Fame three times within seven years, twice as Competitor of the Year and once as Man of the Year. He is now a regular columnist for *Black Belt* and has written three martial arts books: *Karate: Basic Concepts & Skills*, *Dynamic Kicking & Stretching*, and *The Ultimate Kick*. He has also appeared in several movies.

Wallace is one of the most sought-after martial arts clinicians in the world. He lives in St. Petersburg, Florida.

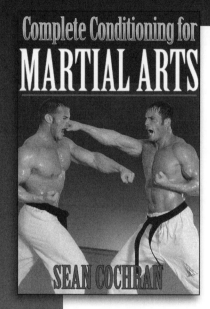